# Joyride

# Joyride

✦

## A Son's Unlikely Journey to His Mother's Heart

*Craig David Forrest*

iUniverse, Inc.
New York  Lincoln  Shanghai

# Joyride
## A Son's Unlikely Journey to His Mother's Heart

iUniverse books may be ordered through booksellers or by contacting:

iUniverse
2021 Pine Lake Road, Suite 100
Lincoln, NE 68512
www.iuniverse.com
1-800-Authors (1-800-288-4677)

ISBN-13: 978-0-595-33816-0 (pbk)
ISBN-13: 978-0-595-78606-0 (ebk)
ISBN-10: 0-595-33816-X (pbk)
ISBN-10: 0-595-78606-5 (ebk)

Printed in the United States of America

This Book Is For:

My mom, who believed that the only one who could tell you how to live was yourself.

My son, who loves to read and will have *Joyride* for his children to read and so on.

And my wife, who shows me every day what real love is.

All the members of the Cape May Beach Patrol and ocean lifeguards around the world who save lives every summer day—you're my heroes.

Everyone that has been touched by either A.L.S or Cancer, thank you for letting me include your stories; for that I will always remember you.

Every friend I've shared the ocean with—to me those days are priceless, and I greatly appreciate our times together.

# *Contents*

# Acknowledgements

First and foremost, I owe much thanks to my mother because she's the central character and without her I would have no story to tell. My deepest appreciation and love go out to my wife, Tara, who listened to every woe and offered the simplest advice that got me through the toughest times of *Joyride*. My deepest thanks goes out to my stepfather, John Moore, who, upon first reading *Joyride*, believed it could be a book and provided valuable editorial advice.

I'm very grateful to author Frank McCourt, who gave my manuscript a good read and offered kind words. Also, thank you to authors Jeanie and James Houston, who gave sound advice while I was conceiving *Joyride*. Thanks also to author Micah Perks, who provided critical suggestions during the early stages of my manuscript. I'm grateful to author Dave Eggers, who stood outside 826 Valencia St. and advised a struggling writer, much like he once was, on publishing. Thank you to my mother's editor, Joe Zelnick, who saw the need to publish family humor columns.

I'm grateful to Dr. Julie Hersch, her team of nurses, and Dr. Sterling Louis, who helped cure me of cancer. There are particular people that have helped along the way that truly believed that *Joyride* was a story worth telling; you know who you are and I'm forever grateful to you. My deepest thank you goes to Angela Rinaldi, my agent, who has been wonderful and constantly reminds what a professional is.

This book would not have been possible without the support of the City of Cape May, New Jersey. Finally, to my father Mark, my two brothers, Keith and Johnny, and my entire extended family, I owe many thanks for their always amazing support.

# *Fishbowl*

Ever wonder what it's like to "grow up in a goldfish bowl"? To always be in the public eye like some English princess? Or the child of a famous movie star? Well, I didn't have to wonder. I grew up in my mom's newspaper column.

My mother wrote a humor column for weekly newspapers. When someone in our family did something noteworthy, she spotlighted it in her column. So, whatever I did that was particularly cute, silly, or stupid showed up in the following week's paper. Week after week, year after year, my life was an open book. My accomplishments—more often my antics—were quickly broadcast to friends, relatives, and neighbors; not to mention teachers, merchants, and police officers. My nuttiest escapades, which were plentiful, became widely known in Cape May, New Jersey, my boyhood hometown.

In her column, my mom never mentioned my name. She referred to me simply as "No. 2." Nevertheless, it seemed to me as if everyone knew No. 2 was *me*. In the column, my older brother, Keith, was similarly named "No. 1." Whenever my mom's first or second husband was mentioned, he was referred to only as "The Hubby."

Before my sixth birthday, I had become an avid reader of my mom's column. My older brother, Keith, and I had to read it, to discover what she wrote about us. It prepared us for the inevitable schoolyard questions and taunts—as well as the occasional compliment.

Imagine having the other kids in your neighborhood read this about your not-long-ago past:

> I was always out in the backyard hanging up diapers. I used to swear my sons would go up the wedding aisle in diapers. I threatened to run away from home if he didn't grow up.
>
> "Leave a little baby like me?" he later asked.
>
> "You were no longer a little baby," I said. "You were running all over the neighborhood, pulling your red wagon around, with your diaper hanging down around your ankles. It was humiliating."
>
> "I was humiliated?" asked No. 2.
>
> "No, you weren't humiliated," I said. "*I* was humiliated. You just went on your merry way, leaving puddles, oblivious to how you were shaming me."
>
> —"Joyride" II, April 28, 1982 (when the author was eleven years old and subject to much schoolyard sarcasm)

Literally thousands of readers laughed at me every week. My misery was their merriment. They smiled at my mom's descriptions of the horrible predicaments I got myself into. They chuckled at some my life's most embarrassing moments. For instance:

> A technician in a white uniform came and got No. 2 and took him with her. I could hear her telling him she was going to give him a blood test. She was calmly and expertly explaining what she was going to do. I could hear No. 2's anxious questions. She kept talking.
>
> And then I heard his piercing scream.
>
> It seemed like a long time before No. 2 came out holding a Kleenex and putting up a good front. But his fright was written all over his face.
>
> —"Joyride" II, March 21, 1979

It had its upside, though, too. Reading my mom's column taught me much. In my later years I came to realize it contained her deepest observations on family life and humanity in general. It reflected her philosophy, which in my adulthood enabled me to escape an early cancerous death and avoid an almost certain nervous breakdown.

Aptly titled *Joyride*, her column chronicled her "Joyride" through life. The column originated before I was born, at the *Southwest Globe-Times*, a Philadelphia neighborhood newspaper of which she, the editor, wrote the column under her maiden name, Libby Demp. A few years after she married my father, Mark Forrest, a popular radio and television journalist, we all moved to Cape May. Here, as Libby Demp Forrest, she became a reporter and columnist for *Wildwood Gazette-Leader*. Later, she graduated to the more widely circulated *Cape May County Herald* group of newspapers. The Herald's editor, Joe Zelnick, told me her column had thousands of avid readers. Just imagine having your dumbest antics broadcast to so many people so quickly!

Imagine having your friends read this about your lack of knowledge about "the facts of life":

> "When will the baby be born?" asked No. 2.
>
> "We don't know," I said. Her water broke at four-thirty this morning."
>
> "Her water broke?" asked No. 2, mystified. "Why doesn't she call a plumber?"
>
> "This has got nothing to do with plumbing," I said.
>
> "It doesn't?" asked No. 2, even more mystified.
>
> "No," I said, "when the water breaks it's a sign the baby's getting started."
>
> "When the pipe broke in the kitchen last summer you didn't have a baby," said No. 2.
>
> —"Joyride II" July 11, 1979

I was born—in the column—while approaching my fifth birthday. It was then (August 31, 1975) that my brother and I first entered into print. "My children have suggested I ought to write a column about them," began the first Gazette-Leader column in which we were mentioned.

No. 2 was the protagonist, constantly providing comedy. No. 1 was the "straight man." No. 1 was conservative, serious, an analytical problem solver.

# Cape May

Mostly, my mom wrote about heartfelt memories—from yesterday or decades past. She rejoiced about raising two boys on a vacation resort island that had a population of three thousand in the winter and quadruple that in the summer.

Cape May is America's oldest seashore resort town. It boasts pristine white beaches, beautiful Victorian houses, and an old-fashioned boardwalk. In those days, it had much to offer a rambunctious boy. Salt-water marshes throughout the island presented many opportunities for fun and adventure. The beach was almost in my backyard. I learned to swim, surf, and lifeguard virtually yards from my home. In the marsh waters, my friends and I sailed everything from plastic bathtubs to old mattresses. We'd have what we called "boat wars."

# *Jailbreak*

The kids I hung around with called my backyard "The Land of the Lost." A boy-sized hole in the fence lattice surrounding our yard opened up to seven adjacent backyards. This was a portal to sheer fun.

My friends said I knew every similar crevice in Cape May. This came from our playing a game we called "Jailbreak," which required finding a good hiding spot. At this game, I was a champion. Almost always, I was last to be found. I'd usually still be hiding behind a bush while the other boys were "held captive" on porches of seasonally deserted summer houses, as my friends called out, "Craig, free us. Craig, Jailbreak us."

> No. 2 came tearing up to me one day after school. "What did you do to the bushes?" he yelled.
>
> "Just trimmed them," I said. "They were years overdue."
>
> "I'm ruined," No. 2 gasped.
>
> "The bushes needed trimming," I repeated. "What does it matter to you?"
>
> "I used to be able to hide behind them," No. 2 said forlornly.
>
> —"Joyride" II, September 24, 1980

We built "forts" in the marshes. Trees, brush, and high grass camouflaged our entryway. When older kids neared our fort, we threw "brains" at them. (This was heavy rotten fruit resembling a hybrid of mutant avocado and animal brains.) We stacked them up, ready to be fired at will. We pretended we owned the town. We considered the older kids invading aliens.

> "We call that 'brains,'" No. 2 said. I could see how a boy's imagination might well give it such a name. "I was never to see that 'fort' again because a few days later some older boys came along and turned it upside down."
> —"Joyride" III, June 15, 1988

Unlike the town's summer residences, our fort wasn't seasonal. All year we anticipated the night before Halloween. Toilet paper was stockpiled during the summer months, hidden beneath our beds. Eggs were collected weeks before, so they would be "nice and rotten." Detailed maps hung on the soggy walls of our fort. Red grids outlined the hot spots where "Coppers" might frequent.

The "Jailbreak" game sometimes got a little out of control, with backyard fences broken, tree limbs ripped off, and occasionally a player getting a bad scratch, bruise, or poke in the eye.

Although some neighbors considered me a disobedient brat, I was very much a "momma's boy." If she yelled "Craig" just once, I'd come running home to 314 Jefferson Street.

For instance, there was the time our "Jailbreak" commotion reached an all-time high. As I lay hidden beneath a shrub, sweat poured off my face and ears. Kids were shouting at the tops of their lungs. Seconds before I was about to make my daring sprint to free everyone, my mom walked out on our front porch and shouted, "The game is over!" Everyone froze, then dispersed with shocked faces. I was defeated. Mom had me call it quits. As usual, when she called, I immediately obeyed. Disappointed and angry, I climbed the brick steps to our front door. Uttering not a word, I simply gave her a red-faced, puzzled stare, as if to say "What? Were we getting out of hand?"

# Mom's Seashore Wisdom

Although it's now a year-round resort, when I was a kid Cape May underwent a dramatic metamorphosis each vacation season, which began on Memorial Day weekend and ended on Labor Day.

> Something happens on the beach. I've never quite understood what it is or what happens to it when summer ends, but I do know that between June and September a lot of people talk to each other who wouldn't be seen dead with one another in November.
>
> Perhaps when people shed some of their clothes they shed some of their prejudices and misconceptions. I am not proclaiming nudity as a means of communication, although it certainly does have its charms after you're eighteen years old and able to vote and licensed to do other things...
> —"Joyride" II, July 6, 1975

Each spring, natives, vacationers, and folks we called "shoebies" suddenly began to bustle around town like hungry bears awakening from winter hibernation, anxious to frolic in the sun. "Shoebies" are tourists who take day trips to the shore. Back then, they often packed their lunch in a shoebox. We slung the word around to insult and deride almost any out-of-towner. We resented their crowding of our island every summer, not to mention their beeping at us from their big cars as we kids rode our bikes toward them down one-way streets.

We proudly referred to ourselves as "locals." Besides actual "shoebies" and "locals," there were numerous vacationers who stayed all season, owning or leasing a Cape May summer home. Others rented a bungalow or apartment for an entire season. There also were a vast number of renters who stayed a week, a few weeks, or even a month. We hurled our "shoebie" insult at all of them.

# *Company Town*

Anyone having a place at the shore tends to become very popular during the season. All of a sudden, my mom would get phone calls and letters from city dwellers wanting to visit.

Mom placed fresh towels for our weekend warriors at the top of the stairway. She then scribbled a note on them that read: *Please use the bath towels for bathing and the beach towels for beaching.* Without fail the bath towels would be caked with sand, lying on the hallway floor, and the beach towels would be hanging nicely on the silver hooks in the bathroom. Late Sunday night, she'd gather the dirty towels. A shriek and then a snicker would ensue when she realized her request was ignored.

> Cape May is what I call a "company town." Oh, I don't mean everybody works at the same factory. What I do mean is that if you have a boat or a house at the shore the world beats a path to your door. "How lucky you are to have a shore place," the company tells you, as they pile luggage in your living room and their dog starts scratching his fleas. Their youngest hands you a plaque she made "just for you" with the word "Daddy" scratched out.
> —"Joyride" II, August 11, 1975

She stayed just one night and used nineteen towels. "She sure took a lot of showers," said No. 2. "How many times did she wash her hair?" asked No. 1. "I think she washed it every hour on the hour," said No. 2.

"At first she only used towels that matched her bathing suit," said No. 2. "But after we ran out of the right colors, she used anything," added No. 1. "She even used my Peanuts towel," said No. 2.

"She took four towels just to go to the beach," said No. 1. "And she didn't even go to the ocean the first afternoon," said No. 2.

"She must think she's Miss Clean or something," said No. 2.

"I don't understand teenage girls," said No. 2.

"Me neither," said No. 1.

"We could write a book about our guests," said No. 2.

"Or a column," said No. 1.

—"Joyride" II, August 8, 1979

Our "company" evaporated as suddenly as it had appeared. Near the end of September, you could feel a cold breeze of loneliness sweeping across the ocean. Merchants hammered plywood over windows to protect their touristy shops from the impending Nor'easter storms. The Family Arcade, The Fudge Kitchen, and Louie's Pizza House turned off their electricity and placed signs on the door that read: "Closed for the winter." The town practically shut down for eight months. As winter neared, the Cape May's maintenance crews swung into action, painting houses, replenishing sand on the beaches, replacing utility polls, digging up and then paving streets, etc. Sometimes, much to the chagrin of the workmen, that opened up opportunities for us kids to have fun.

No. 2 and I have slightly different views of the Frog Hollow sewer installations now in progress. To me, the work underway means mud, noise and roadblocks. To No. 2, the City of Cape May has extended its recreation program to our front door.

"How long do you think all those gigantic cement pipes will be piled up and down Jefferson Street," asked No. 2.

"Why?" I asked.

"Because they're fun to crawl through!" said No. 2.
—"Joyride" II, April 2, 1980

Cape May's rustic saltwater marsh and grassy fields provided me many opportunities to ponder the town's numerous natural wonders. From time to time, I closely observed the winds, the clouds, the ocean, the ponds, the cape's numerous and varicolored birds—and the occasional reptile.

"George" was a box turtle No. 2 carried home one night after a Little League game.

"I found him in the field behind the school," No. 2 said. "I saved him from the other players. I'm going to let him stay here."

No. 2 went in search of a cardboard box. He got scissors and used them to cut up grass for the box. He found a glass desert dish and filled it with water.

Then he moved George into the box.

"Look at him," No. 2 observed, "he's smiling."

I studied George and did detect a slight smile on the turtle's face.

Days later: "It must be 100 degrees out on the porch," I said.

I went and took a look at George. His home was a mess. The water dish was turned over. The grass was all dried out. The vegetables had turned brown. I had a talk with No. 2.

"George is a creature of nature," I said. "He's meant to live free. You love your freedom, don't you? I think George does too."

He walked and walked, then scrambled under a wire fence to release George.

"I put George behind the fence," said No. 2 when he returned, "so the players won't bother him. Maybe I'll see him again someday watching the games."

—"Joyride" II, July 6, 1983

Whether the topic was a tattered home for George or my bad attitude toward her stopping play for dinner, Mom rarely hesitated to speak her mind in print about my escapades and peccadilloes. No matter how personal, she seemed to write whatever suited her fancy about my brother and me. For instance, what kid wants the whole town to read about his underwear?

Underwear is a dirty word around our house. I am not allowed to use it.

Dirty underwear is another dirty word; even dirtier, in fact.

It seems children must go through stages where certain words become taboo, and at this moment "underwear" is an X-rated word I am trying to avoid using at all costs.

But, sometimes, even I slip.

The other day I was folding laundry and when I had a pile of that X-rated word together I asked No. 2 to take it upstairs. I momentarily forgot that underwear is a dirty word nowadays and I asked No. 2 to take the pile upstairs and put it in his underwear drawer.

"Mom," he said "you didn't have to say that word, did you?"

"What word?" I asked innocently.

"You're not going to get me to repeat that word, Mom. I just won't do it."

"You mean u-n-d-e-r-w-e-a-r?"

"Spelling it out is just as bad, Mom."

"I still don't see what's wrong with using THAT word. It's not like cussing."

"It just embarrasses me, Mom. I wish you wouldn't use it."

"Well would you take this pile of garments that are worn underneath your outer clothes upstairs to your room and put them in the second drawer from the top where unmentionables are until used?"

"Okay, Mom, that's better."

"And while you're at it, would you mind crawling under your bed and retrieving the other unmentionables that you throw under it when you are changing dirty unmentionables for clean unmentionables?"

"I don't always throw my hummmmph under the bed."

*"Most of the time you throw your hummmmph under the bed."*

"A lot of the time I put my hummmmph in the laundry hamper."

"Not too often, I'd say. Every time I do the laundry I have to crawl around under the bed and look for your dirty hummmmph. Sometimes I have to get the broom to push it out it's so far under the bed."

"Mom, when I'm in a hurry to get to school in the morning I can't always remember to put my hummmmph in the hamper."

"Well, you have to walk right by it in order to go out your bedroom door. There's no other way to get out of your room unless you climb out the window."

"Okay, okay, Mom."

He came downstairs a few minutes later carrying a basket of dirty underwear and stuffed it into the washing machine before I could sort it.

"Hey hold on there," I said, "I like to sort out the hummmmph before I wash it."

"You mean you have to look at it?"

"Sure, why not?"

"That's revolting," No. 2 said.

"Look I said I didn't invent this job. If you want to wash your own hummmmph, that's okay with me. I need all the help I can get."

"It's not that I don't trust you, Mom," No. 2 said, "it's just that my own hummmmph is my own business."

—"Joyride" February 8, 1981 (when the author was ten years old)

Embarrassment became a routine. After that column was published I went on a rampage, running from one newsstand to another, hoping to rid the town of every newspaper that ran Mom's column. For a whole week, it seemed as if almost every literate fifth-grader chased me around the schoolyard calling me "Underwear Boy." By the time I got rid of that nickname, thanks to the column, I got a new one the following week.

My mom had a wonderful sense of humor. She usually didn't take herself too seriously. She was as quick to demean herself in print as she was her offspring. In her *"Joyride"* column, humiliation was a family affair:

There's a new kid on the block who tells it like he sees it. I'm not sure if I like him. The other day he came into our house uninitiated for the first time.

"This place looks like *The Amityville Horror*," he said.

"What's your name?" I asked him.

"Ralph," he said.

"That's a dumb name," I said.

"Boy this house is something," he said.

"Did you move here from Plasticville?" I asked.

"Why do you save old newspapers?" Ralph asked.

"Because we're smart enough to be able to read them," I said.

"How come there's a hole in the ceiling?" Ralph asked.

"It's for Santa Claus," I said, "so he doesn't have to get singed coming down the chimney."

"This house is something," Ralph repeated.

"We give tours as a sideline," I said.

"How can you see out those windows?" Ralph asked.

"We don't like sunlight," I said. "I turn into a vampire if too much sun filters through."

"You have such funny looking plants over there," said Ralph. "They look like they're dead."

"They're a special species that don't like water."

"They still look dead to me," Ralph said.

"Ralph," I said, "why don't you go home?"

> "Boy this house is really something," Ralph said again. "How come you have that rug rolled up on top of the carpet in the living room?"
>
> "Because," I said.
>
> "I've never been in a house that looked like this," Ralph said.
>
> "You haven't lived," I said. "Why don't you go home?"
>
> —"Joyride" September 26, 1979

I didn't appreciate her writing about our family life, but I didn't hold it against her. I mean, sure, I sometimes yelled and complained to her about my life in a "fishbowl," but she always was a great mother to me—and I tried my best to be a good son. What I mean by "a good son" is that even as a small boy I did more than merely take out the trash every week. My brother and I did our share of household chores. Many times in a single parent household you begin to feel that you're not merely a son but also the man of the house. That's the case even when you have an older brother. Being the "man" can be a lot of work for a nine-year-old. From time to time, I listened sympathetically to my mom's problems and offered her kid advice.

> No. 2 is everybody's friend. He's a good listener and a good consoler, peacemaker, and rescuer. Sometimes I think he was born sixty-five years old.
>
> The other night he caught me unaware. I was feeling blue. "Cheer up," No. 2 said to me. "What's the problem?"
>
> I just stared off into space.
>
> "Isn't it better to talk about it?" asked No. 2. He sat down beside me, his big blue eyes searching mine. "Whatever is bothering you, try to forget it," he suggested.
>
> "I can't," I said.
>
> "Think of it this way," he said, "Pretend your mind is a blackboard."
>
> "Okay," I agreed. "I'll pretend my mind is a blackboard."

"Now take an eraser and erase whatever is on the black-board," he said.

—"Joyride" II, June 27, 1979 (when the author was eight years old)


A child psychiatrist of sorts, the idea of helping people was really my forte. I dreamed about being that hero—you know the type—who runs through a burning farmhouse to rescue a child. I remember staging elaborate make-believe rescue situations with my toy fire trucks.

One day when I was eight, on the beach I noticed a boy sitting on the lifeguard stand alongside "real lifeguards." He wore a minia-ture uniform, and around his neck was a worn-out shoelace string that held a whistle. "I want to do that," I hollered.

"Do what?" Mom asked.

"That," I said, pointing over her shoulder toward the mini-life-guard. She squinted as the sun shone into her eyes, and for a brief moment we stared together at that little guy as I envisioned myself in his place in the near future.


"Got to go now, Mom," said No. 2. "I have to report for duty."

It is summer now, at which time No. 2 gives up the silly life of a schoolboy and commences the serious work of a lifeguard mascot.

"A couple of years from now, I'm going to be a lifeguard," says No. 2, "but I've got a lot to learn in the meantime."

To hear No. 2 tell it, he's practically a lifeguard now. "After all," says No. 2, "this is my third year as a mascot."

What do mascots do?

"I run a lot of errands," says No. 2. "The lifeguards get hun-gry a lot."

"Then you're well qualified to be a lifeguard," I say.

"We help keep the beaches clean," says No. 2. "Get rid of pieces of wood that float in. Stuff like that."

"How come you help to keep the beach clean, then run home and throw your sneakers in the middle of the living room floor?" I ask.

"You don't understand," says No. 2.

"I guess not," I say. "I'm just a mother."

"I can handle a whistle now. I'm learning to study the waves. I'm in charge of watching the equipment," says No. 2.

"How are you with girls?" I ask.

"That comes with the job," says No. 2.

"Don't lifeguards get to study the girls as much as they study the waves?" I ask.

"It might seem that way," says No. 2. "Actually I'm a big help to the lifeguards in that way."

"How come?" I ask.

"I help to get them dates," says No. 2.

"Come on now," I say. "A kid like you? Those great big handsome guys need a kid like you to help them get dates?"

"I make introductions. I give messages. I size up girls by talking to them first, then go back to the lifeguards and tell them what I've found out," says No. 2.

"What do you find out?" I ask.

"Number one: Are they single? Sometimes a terrific looking girl comes to the beach with a little baby and the lifeguards may wonder if she's babysitting the kid. I have to find out if it's her kid or not," says No. 2.

"I see," I say.

"Sometimes the girls are going with some guy and the lifeguards don't want to get involved with that. So I find out for them if the girls are available or not," says No. 2.

"Important," I say.

"Believe it or not, even though the lifeguards are good-looking guys, some of them are even shy. So, I have to help them," says No. 2.

"Responsibility," I comment.

No. 2 nods.

"The only thing is," says No. 2, "by the time I become a lifeguard, where am I going to find another mascot like me?"

—"Joyride" July 17, 1982

# Santa Cruz and Tara

Presently, my home is on the Pacific Coast, near Santa Cruz, California. Now married, with a son, the three of us travel back to Cape May each summer. My wife, Tara, and I enjoy returning to New Jersey, where we both work as Cape May Beach Patrol lifeguards.

No. 2 son fell in love with the seashore when he was five months old. He crawled to the water's edge and would have kept going had we let him.

I always said he was born part fish.

This year he and his bride of two years returned from California, and they're working for the summer on the Cape may beach patrol.

You see, when the fish person grew up, he married the mermaid of his dreams.

—"Joyride" III, July 16, 1997

They look good together, there's no denying that. He, with that thrust of blond hair and huge grin; she, dark-haired and dark-eyed, with enigmatic smile.

And they treat one another with consideration and good humor. I hear them laughing together and I think to myself, That's a very good sign. Give them a plus for the willingness to laugh at the absurdities of life. There will be, I can assure them, many laughs and many absurdities, along with many events they won't find much to laugh about.

—"Joyride" III, August 3, 1994

However, the main reason we went east soon after moving to the West Coast wasn't a pleasurable one. We went to help care for my mom, who was suffering from a terribly debilitating illness.

# Columns in the Attic

During my adult years, I often went up to the attic of my mom's house to relive my fondest *Joyride*s. That's where she kept her old files. Rereading them was a kind of therapy for me. Amidst trunks, antiques, assorted junk, and old books, I reviewed her prose line by line, reliving memories and reexamining my life.

She wrote more than twelve hundred columns. Sometimes I felt I could learn more about her by reading her columns than by conversing with her. They chronicled her life, from before my brother and I were born, up to her last few weeks. Her columns were a platform for her philosophy, whether she was writing about her childhood in West Philadelphia, her failed first marriage, differences between her sons, or aspects of seashore living. She relished writing about her life and our lives. As I reread her old columns, I remembered her humor, her strength, her youthfulness. As I read on, my troubles tended to disappear.

When I heard she was seriously ill, I promptly flew from the West Coast to Philadelphia. Here, my father (nicknamed "The Ayatollah" by my mother) met me at the airport. Balding and stout, he was mourning the recent death of his second wife. Though we never were emotionally close, we hugged. We zoomed away to his stately Swarthmore home, where he loaned me one of his cars, a beautiful big black Cadillac, to drive myself to Marmora, New Jersey, about forty-five miles north of Cape May. Recently released from the hospital, my mother was at a rehabilitation center there.

En route to New Jersey, I drove across the Walt Whitman Bridge, named for one of my mother's favorite writers. Every time we crossed that bridge, she would recite some of his poetry. One time, she passionately explained what a transcendentalist was and how living for life is much better than living for money. My mom was a closet New Age transcendentalist—concerned only with the honey that life had to offer. I hung on every word she said, wanting more but never asking for it.

# Jersey Devil

After driving for about an hour, I knew I was lost. As usual, I took directions half-assed. I figured I'd somehow—perhaps cosmically—find where I needed to be. The Caddy was getting hot, so I decided to pull over and look at a map. I've been in this area a thousand times, I thought.

According to what I saw on the map, I seemed to be in the Jersey Pine Barrens, the home of the Jersey Devil of folklore. In seventh grade, I'd gone on a three-day camping trip in these foreboding woods. Thirty pimply-faced kids nibbled on potato chips and other snacks while carrying sleeping bags and camping gear. Some of the kids brought along magnifying glasses to examine bugs that we encountered during our hikes.

A medium security prison was on the outskirts. The camp counselors threatened incarceration there whenever we exhibited bad behavior. From day one, we hikers anticipated the promised night hike, not only because we expected it to be lots of fun, but because it was also an opportunity to see the legendary Jersey Devil.

> "I hope the Jersey Devil is ready for you," I said to No.2 as I helped roll up the sleeping bag.
> "Come on Mom," said No.2, "you're just trying to scare me."
> —"Joyride" III, April 17, 1985

Overflowing with nervous energy, we began our hike at dusk. The counselors told us someone had sighted the Devil earlier that day. As we walked a three-mile loop, the counselors went ahead. Suddenly, they jumped out of the bushes, screaming: "The Jersey Devil is here." They scared the living crap out of us. When we got back to the cabin, we all realized no one had really seen any legendary monster.

Earlier, around a campfire, we'd heard how the Jersey Devil was the thirteenth offspring of someone named Mother Leeds. She supposedly gave birth during a big storm—rain, hail, tornadoes, and all that gnarly stuff—to a dog-faced, winged, dragon-like creature that ate her other twelve kids. To this day, backwoods folk in the Pine Barrens talk about a cackling, tail-whipping monster who tromps through the backyards of trailer parks or ravages campsites.

When we returned from our night hike, we found that someone had broken into our cabin. A counselor called the state park rangers. Two windows had been knocked out on the second floor. The rangers examined the cabin with their big flashlights, as we stood outside terrified. I was thoroughly convinced the Jersey Devil had come to eat every one of us.

I stood there, my mouth agape. Wild fantasies materialized. I envisioned high-pitched squeals and rangers being hurled out of the cabin, bloodied and disoriented. I imagined myself grabbing one of those big flashlights and yelling, "I'll take care of this!" In my daydream, I entered the cabin and head-locked the Jersey Devil, tightly squeezing his pointed head, to the applause of my classmates and counselors.

In reality, the rangers came and informed us that an escaped convict had broke into the cabin and grabbed someone's sleeping bag and flashlight. We sighed when we heard the news. To us, it was much more reassuring to hear that there was an escaped convict loose in the Pine Barrens than the child-eating Jersey Devil.

# *Rehab*

After the Caddy cooled down, I drove east on U.S. Route 40 and found the rehabilitation center. Approaching slowly, it was as if I was casing the joint. It was a hot evening, and I was sweaty and pulsing with nervous energy. The setting sun was a bright orange ball, reminding me I wasn't on the West Coast but in New Jersey, where summer nights can be almost as hot as the days. Apparently I was at the rear of the rehab complex. Rusty metal hospital beds without mattresses were stacked outside.

Anxiously pulling on the handle of the back door, I accidentally set off an alarm. Ignoring the clamor, I quickly walked up and down the halls calling out, "Mom." As alarms rang in the background, I said it louder and louder.

A young nurse with short black hair and drowsy eyes approached and asked, "May I help you?" I took a step backward and thought, Yeah, I do need help; mental help. I'm freaking out inside. I need a hug. I'm having a really rough time. Will you just…hold me?

Instead, I muttered, "Yeah, I'm sorry, I triggered the alarm because…"

She motioned down the hallway and said, "I know. What's your mother's name?"

"Uhh…Libby Demp Forrest Moore."

(My mom had four names. She used them in various combinations at different times. My mother said she liked all three surnames and felt that each defined some important aspect of her personality and period in her life. She seemed to wear them like medals of honor or scout merit badges.)

The nurse gingerly walked away from me and exclaimed, "I'll go up to the front desk and find her room number for you."

"Okay," I responded.

Then I began going to every room, one by one, opening each door and peering inside. Luckily, the sixth room I checked contained my sleeping mother. "Mom," I said in a sort of loud whisper. "Mom, Mom," I said louder, not shouting, in a sort of coffee shop conversation voice. Her eyes opened. "Craig, how's it going?"

"Good. Not so good for you?" was my answer and question within the same breath.

"They told me I'll be home in two days," she said, making me wonder, "Are they just telling her that? Or is she really coming home?"

She looked up at me and said, "It will be hard for me to get around." Referring to my stepfather, she added, "John knew you were coming today, so he ordered a new rug to be delivered tomorrow. The one we have now is too thick for the wheelchair. Maybe you can get a friend to help you pull the old rug up?"

"Sure, no problem," I assured her.

Mom grabbed the bed sheet and smiled, "I'm really happy you're here. Will you be around a while?"

"Yep, I'll be here for about five weeks, just trying to help out," I replied.

"Great. That sounds great, Craigie," she exclaimed, using the nickname which she often called me in person but never in the column.

# *Unruly Behavior*

The next morning I drove the black beauty down U.S. Route 9 and the Garden State Parkway. On the parkway, Cape May is exit zero. "The end of the world," my mom often said, because the next town straight ahead is Dingle, Ireland, on the other side of the Atlantic Ocean.

Driving over a small bridge, past a marina and the famous Lobster House at the town's entrance, my car cruised down Washington Street. Each time I return to Cape May, I revisit my childhood. The Caddy was smoking again, and I was glad to be almost "home." On my right was my old elementary school, where my mom had made numerous visits to the principal's office.

A story she enjoyed telling was when, during bone-chilling December weather, I took off my winter jacket and flung it onto the school's roof to the chanting dares of my classmates. To retrieve my jacket, Mr. Giddings, the school's sixty-year-old janitor, climbed a creaky old ladder up to the roof. As he threw my jacket down to me, we watched in horror as he slipped down the ladder rung by rung. He sprained his ankle. After being grabbed by the ear, I was dragged to the office of the principal, who promptly called my mom and told her about my unruly behavior. This wasn't the first nor last such call from the principal's office. Each time, she'd ride her three-wheel bike up Jefferson Street and down Lafayette Street, four blocks total, to the front door of the school. On the way home, she'd make me walk next to her as she rode—my three steps to her one pedal. Usually, she would not speak to me until hours later.

# Wrestling With Bob

When No. 2 son called, he was surprised I had bought a new rug. "Didn't you just buy one not so long ago, Mom?" he asked.

"That was fifteen years ago," I informed him.

—"Joyride" III, November 9, 1994

Professionals were coming to deliver and install new carpeting to accommodate my mom's wheelchair, walker, etc. Before their arrival, the old floor coverings had to be removed. For some reason, I had assured everyone that I would have helpers to remove all the furniture and old floor coverings from two large downstairs rooms before the pros showed up. I didn't. Instead, I had to struggle by myself all day with heavy furniture and cumbersome rugs. As the day wore on and I wore out, I called Tara, my wife in California, and moaned, "I'm drained. I can't do this anymore."

"You can do this," she assured me. "You're strong."

Trying not to cry, I went back to pulling and lifting and grunting. It didn't want to come up. After hours of work, only one cubic foot was removed. Chiseling through, sweating on, and cussing at it, I decided that rug was an enemy with a brutal strength and stubbornness of its own. He is, I thought, an enemy named Bob. Why it was named Bob, I didn't know. Up till then, everyone I had met named Bob seemed pretty decent. But this Bob was a real prick, big and stubborn. I tried to reason with him but he paid no attention. I yelled at him but it had no effect. So I decided, as an amateur wrestler of some experience, simply to whip his ass. And—I did. Soon enough, the defeated Bob was out of the house. "Good riddance, Bob!" I shouted.

The carpet pros showed up promptly at nine o'clock the next morning. I asked one if he could take care of Bob. He looked at me as if I was nuts. Thinner and smaller than me, he carried Bob's replacement on his shoulder like he was carrying a case of beer. In a few hours, the new carpeting was laid out nicely on the hardwood floor. Instead of Bob's ugly beige, there was soothing blue. Bob's replacement will be nice to mom's wheelchair, I thought.

After the carpet guys departed, mom's "hubby" called and informed me, "Your mother is coming home tomorrow." My cheerful reply: "Great, the new rug is here," as if the past day's travail had never happened. On his way home from work in Washington, my stepdad picked up my mom at the rehab center and drove her to Cape May.

# Surfing to Escape

Usually, rather than wrestling with troublesome rugs, in times of stress I go surfing. At such times, surfing is my refuge, my escape. Of course, when I'm feeling good, I also surf. Surfing has always been there for me during the worst and best of times. At this particular moment, however, my surfboard was in Santa Cruz, three thousand miles away as the crow flies, while a tropical storm was swirling in the Atlantic, generating great surfing waves.

I sat hypnotized, watching TV. A colorful Weather Channel graph plotted Tropical Storm Opal off Cape Hatteras, North Carolina. "The Eastern Seaboard should get substantial swell in the upward of ten feet for the next couple days," the TV weather reporter said.

I figured the waves were good. While I'd struggled with Bob days before, I saw people pass our house carrying surfboards to the beach.

So, I walked there myself to check out the waves, and ran into a blonde-bearded old friend named Evan. He lives in Colorado in the wintertime and lifeguards in Cape May in the summer. We talked for a few minutes on his lifeguard stand. Surfers streamed past in a blur as we discussed my mom's condition and the skiing he'd done the last winter.

"You should get out there; the waves are going off," Evan suggested.

"I'd love to, but my board is back in California," I lamented.

"I have a board my sister gave me," he said. "You're welcome to use it. It's in my backyard underneath the porch."

"What kind of board is it?" I asked.

"I'm not sure," he answered.

Evan isn't a surfing freak. For him, surfing is more or less a novelty. I graciously accepted Evan's offer and wandered barefoot toward his place. Evan was staying at a summer rental with four other lifeguards two blocks away from my mom's house. I entered the backyard and saw the board. It was old and full of holes. Black and neon pink; probably made in the early eighties, I thought. I grabbed the board under my arm and walked back toward the beach. My feet burned on the hot asphalt. Sweat poured down on my new borrowed gift. I walked past Evan's stand, gave him a thumbs-up, and paddled out into the ocean.

The current was moving fast. Before I knew it, I was two rock piles over and heading toward Steger Beach, a really good surfing spot. A set of waves approached me and I paddled hard for the first one. My hands burned in the salt water because of blisters acquired while wrestling Bob. I felt the wave pick up the board. I stood up and crouched back down a little bit. The wave was hollow and a few feet overhead. My fingers grazed the face of the wave and I got deeper into the tube. I drove for the blazing sun as the lip got heavier. A few seconds later I was spit out from the wave. A famous pro surfer from South Africa once said, "Time stands still in the tube." He was definitely right. For that moment, my mother's illness and all my anxiety disappeared. At that very moment, nothing mattered except that I was surfing.

# *Homecoming*

The following day, my stepfather, The Hubby, pulled up the long driveway with mom in the front seat. Running out to greet them, I shouted, "Mom, you're home. I'm so happy." Her face seemed tired. Darkness encircled her eyes. Visibly upset, my stepdad snapped, "The new rug is in?"

"Yeah, it looks great," I replied.

"Okay, fine, let's get Libby into the wheelchair," he continued.

"The wheelchair?" I asked.

"The wheelchair," he repeated. "She needs the wheelchair. That's why we got the new rug, so the wheelchair could roll on it properly."

"Oh yeah, that's right," I confirmed, reaching to help lift her from the front seat of his little Ford Escort. We lifted her into a wheelchair the rehab center had lent her to use until her own was delivered. After wheeling her to the brick steps, we suddenly realized we couldn't get the wheelchair up without another person. Adjusting his tie, The Hubby decided, "We need help; we can't do this by ourselves."

I quickly thought of all my friends in the neighborhood who might be available to help, and concluded they all were working on the beach.

Maybe a neighbor, I thought. Maybe a passerby, but they need to be strong. Glancing at my mom, I said, "I'll be right back."

I ran across the street to the Murphy family's house and knocked on their door. A young man wearing a swimsuit opened it and asked, "Yes?"

To which I promptly replied, "My mom just came back from the hospital and we need some help to get her up the steps. She's in a wheelchair."

He reacted instantly. "Sure, hold on," he said. "Dad, I'm going to help the people across the street. Okay? Okay, let's go."

As we crossed the street, his father, in his sixties, quickly followed. Two of us got on each side of the wheelchair and together we said, "One, two, three, four, lift." She was in the air like the queen of Africa. When we approached the third step, with nine more to go, I noticed tears running down her face. "Mom, are you okay?" I asked.

"I'm fine," she said. Personally, I think she was overwhelmed that these neighbors had come so readily to her assistance. Or maybe she was just so glad to be home.

Eventually we reached the top and took her inside. The Hubby took a white handkerchief from his pocket, wiped his brow, let out a loud sigh, and said, "Thank you very much for all your help." My mom said nothing as she wiped her tears away with the backs of her hands.

For many years, she was free as a bird to roam throughout this house. Two stories high, it contained ten rooms, plus two large third-floor attic rooms, and front and back porches. Now she was very limited as to where she could go, confined to the first floor. It took time to adjust to the new living arrangements. The laundry room was now her bathroom. It was the only place on the first floor with both a sink and a toilet. Because she couldn't get to the master bedroom on the second floor, a hospital bed delivered that morning was set on the new carpet for her arrival. French doors in the living room gave her a good view of the street and the passing pedestrians and vehicles. These four big doors opened wide to allow her wheel-chair easy access to the front porch. Birds loved this porch because she made sure there always was plenty of birdseed in their feeders. Individual birdbaths were on each side of the porch.

> Are you perhaps wondering what to give to a friend or relative who can't get out; maybe someone who is ill and stuck in bed?
>
> Think about a birdfeeder. A nice gift for a friend; a nice gift for the birds.
>
> Along with the feeder, a beautiful note telling your house-bound friend to await flying lessons.
>
> —"Joyride" II, November 13, 1996

On the day following her homecoming, she lay on her bed in the living room, which now had become her bedroom.

She watched me scrape and sand the eight-foot pillars that held up the porch roof. I'd perform mime routines for her through the glass windows. Sometimes she'd laugh, and she always smiled. I wanted the porch to be nice for her so she could roll out on her wheelchair and breathe the summer air, smell the summer flowers, and remember that life still has many wonders to offer someone even if they are in a wheelchair.

# *Dinner for Two*

Each day, I sanded and scraped until my hands were bloodied. At night we'd make dinner: Anything she wanted. "You want Mexican tonight?" I asked.

"Sure, what kind of Mexican?" she responded.

"How about fajitas?" I said.

"Sounds good. Can you make fajitas?" she asked.

"Can I make fajitas? Don't forget, I'm from California" I told her.

"You're from Jersey; you're not from California," she remarked.

"So, now I live in California, and I know how to make fajitas," I assured her.

"Craig, a few years ago, you didn't even know what an avocado was," she reminded me.

"So?" I said.

"So, you're no expert in Mexican cuisine. You're just lucky you have a wonderful wife who was raised in Mexican surroundings. If she was here, she'd vouch for the fact that I tried for months to get you to eat an avocado."

"So?" I shrugged.

"Never mind," she said, smiling.

The first words out of his mouth every evening: "What's for dinner? Well, I don't want it."

While No. 1 son sat down and attacked his meal, No. 2 son would sit staring at us, his fork playing with his food.

"What's in this?" he asked suspiciously of everything that contained more than one ingredient.

—"Joyride" III, March 4, 1992

"What are we having for dinner, Mom?" asked No. 2.

"Oh, let me think," I said. "Maybe a typical California salad, some sourdough bread, and something grilled. How does that sound?"

"Sourdough bread?" sneered No. 2.

"People in California like that," I replied.

"But we don't here in New Jersey," said No. 2. "It tastes funny."

—"Joyride" II, September 5, 1984

"What are you cooking?" No. 2 asked the other day when he found me throwing some noodles into the slow cooker.

"It's a new dish I found in a recipe book," I said. "Oh," said No. 2, "I'm allergic to it."

"How do you know you're going to be allergic to it when we've never eaten it before?" I asked as I stirred.

—"Joyride" II, June 23, 1982

"I think we should have hoagies for dinner," said No. 2.

I deliberated for a moment. "Italian or American?" I asked. "I'm in the mood for foreign food," said No. 2. "Let's get Italian hoagies."

—"Joyride" II, July 7, 1982

# California Coolness

My mother once wrote a tongue-in-cheek column about me return-ing from California with wild ideas, such as suggesting she vacuum the living room rug while wearing roller blades, wear a headband, and serve only health food. In writing her column, she employed poetic license, exaggerating incidents in which I was involved, such as portraying me as a convert to Californian weirdness.

Easterners do tend to treat Californians as oddballs, cultists, mys-tics, and iconoclasts who continually rub elbows with film stars and movie moguls. When I mention in New Jersey that I live in Califor-nia, people envision me sipping cappuccino alongside Tom Cruise. They think Santa Cruz is only moments away from Hollywood and the Los Angeles beaches. Actually, from where I live, it takes me about eight hours to drive to L.A. I have to keep telling them, "No, there is not an earthquake every day," "No, I can't introduce you to Jennifer Lopez," and "No, we don't eat only Mexican food."

Among Cape May's young summer beach crowd, my living in Santa Cruz seems to signify that I'm either an inspired guru or an enlightened oceanographer. Either way, they envision me as possess-ing special knowledge of the ocean, the winds, aquatic life, and the environment in general. However, my old friends and especially my mom saw me as the same "Craigie" who got himself into so many goofy scrapes in years past.

Sometimes, old buddies came west. At six o'clock one evening, I got a telephone call from two Cape May friends driving big rigs from Jersey to California. "Hey Craig, this is your buddy Doug," stated the voice on the other end of the line. "Me and Joey Pazanski are in Salinas right now. We'd like to hook up with you."

My prompt reply: "Cool, Tara and I will make you guys dinner."

After giving directions and hanging up, I informed my Tara that friends from Cape May were coming for dinner. She and I made guacamole, diced up tomatoes, jalapenos, romaine lettuce, and shredded Monterey jack cheese. An open can of refried beans was set on the stove. Our trucker guests arrived promptly within the hour. These guys are no longer mere Cape May Elementary students, but real grown-up tractor-trailer drivers. Since I was anxious to show I was now a real Californian, I showed off my many surfboards and dished out the native food.

> For awhile No. 2 son, California Man, is honoring us with a visit. We eat alfalfa sprouts for lunch and avocados with dinner. When I used to ask No. 2 son what he wanted for dinner, he'd say, 'A cheese steak.' Not anymore. Now it's 'Fajitas, Mom.'"
>
> So out to the grocery store I go for lime juice, refried beans, and cilantro. This is for a kid who used to turn up his nose at anything other than peanut butter and jelly sandwiches. Now he wants red onions in his salad, balsamic vinegar, and chopped almonds on his rice…
>
> Now he discusses California wines as readily as he once knew only milk, orange juice, and Kool Aid.
> —"Joyride" III, July 21, 1993

The guacamole stood alone on the table in a glass bowl. I took a big wooden spoon and dished it onto my plate. Joey's eye's bulged. In a heavy Jersey accent, he asked loudly, "What's that?" It reminded me that when we were kids, he often yelled.

Pointing proudly at the green stuff, I chuckled, "That? Oh, that's guacamole."

"What is gok-a-mo-lally?" he demanded.

"You've never had guacamole?" I asked.

"No, it looks disgusting," Joey replied.

"Boy," I said, "you haven't lived if you haven't had guacamole."

"Is it good?" he asked.

"Is it good? The best! I can't believe you've never had guacamole!"

"I think I have heard of it," he said. "Yeah I've heard of it. It's at Denny's. Yeah, that's right. I've heard of it before. Matter of fact, I'll get the guacamole burger when I go to Denny's sometimes."

Tara asked him if he liked guacamole. "I don't know..." he said, rubbing his chin.

"What do you mean, 'You don't know'? I thought you said you've ordered the guacamole burger at Denny's?" demanded Tara.

"That's right," he declared.

"How can you order a guacamole burger and not eat the guacamole?" she asked.

"I get it on the side," said Joey.

"You get it on the side?"

"Yeah, I get it on the side. But I don't eat it."

Somewhat befuddled by his replies, she asked, "Why do you get it on the side? Why don't you just get a regular burger without guacamole?"

"Because the Guacamole Burger has Canadian bacon on it," he declared.

"Oh, well that explains it," she shrugged.

Although I sometimes think of myself as a pretty bright guy, my mother always let me know I still had a lot to learn:

> "Are you bringing us back something from your trip, Mom?" asked No.2.
>
> "I suppose," I said absentmindedly as I stuffed my suitcase.
>
> "I could use a new surfboard," said No. 2.
>
> "What I had in mind was a little souvenir," I said. "But California is the place to buy surfboards," said No. 2.

"Rest assured," I said, "you will not see me getting off the plane carrying a surfboard…"

"Mom can only carry so much," said No. 1.

"Hmmm…" said No. 2. "Well, instead of a surfboard, do you think you could get me something else?"

"What's that?" I asked.

"A new wetsuit," said No. 2. "That wouldn't take up much room in your suitcase."

"But a lot of room in my wallet," I said.

—"Joyride" II, August 15, 1984

# *Fatherly Advice*

Near the end of the Cape May sojourn, as I prepared to return to Santa Cruz, I talked with mom about my plans to come back in the summertime. At that time, in California, Tara and I owned a restaurant business. Actually, it was a sandwich shop. It kept my wife and I almost constantly occupied, except for the periodic surfing break. So, I guess I was telling my mom that I *might* be back in the summer.

My stepdad then drove me to the Philadelphia airport, a two-hour trip. Up the Garden State Parkway we passed shore town after shore town. It was Friday afternoon and a steady stream of cars and buses loaded with vacationers and fun seekers passed, going in the opposite direction. We seemed to be the only car heading north. I shuffled my flip-flops off my feet and spurted out, "I'm coming back this summer, with Tara."

"Do you think that's practical?" he asked.

"I think so," I replied.

"What about the restaurant," he said, not so much asking a question as making a comment.

"We'll have someone run it," I assured him, expressing the confidence of someone who usually considers himself, as I said before, "a pretty bright guy."

"Can you find someone who will care for your business the way you would?" he inquired.

"Sure," I snapped.

"Really," he mused, again exclaiming more than questioning. "Well, I think so," I said.

"Just remember," he explained, "nobody will care for something of yours the way you would care for it. It's your business. It's your baby. No hired person is going to give it the tender loving care you and Tara give it. Don't forget that."

As he dropped me off at the airport's Northwest Airlines entrance, we briefly hugged and he rubbed the top of my head.

Back in Santa Cruz, I didn't miss a beat. Back at the restaurant. Back in the water surfing. Didn't miss a beat. I noticed, though, that Tara seemed miserable. The five weeks I was away had worn her down. She had to work unreal hours. She was visibly exhausted. Though she recognized I had gone to Cape May for a noble reason, Tara resented having to shoulder one hundred percent of the responsibility for our business.

Despite our desire to hold down our phone bills, we called mom often. Being disabled, she used a speaker telephone. In those days, coast-to-coast telecommunication wasn't all that good. It often was difficult to hear mom, let alone understand what she was saying. After two or three minutes, I'd ask to talk with my stepdad. He gave me the latest word on the state of her health. His reports were a medical student's dream and a son's nightmare. Her condition continuously and steadily worsened. It progressed almost exactly as predicted.

Except for my mom's woes, my West Coast life up to that time was fairly enjoyable. Among other benefits, I had, here in California, my own business; a beautiful, talented, devoted wife; a bright and adoring son who surfed; and a handsome golden retriever. Outweighing all this was how much I sorely missed my mother. Off and on, the words of my stepdad on the way to the airport rang in my head: "Nobody will care for something of yours the way you will…."

Somebody you hire won't give it the tender loving care you and Tara give it."

I made up my mind. "Tara," I declared, "we're closing down shop."

"What do you mean?" she asked.

"I mean, I can't listen to mom on the speakerphone any more, knowing I can't do anything for her. I can't pretend I'm living happily out here while she's suffering back there. That's living a lie."

"Why a lie?" she asked.

"Because I'm not being true to myself, to mom, to you."

"To me? Why me?"

"Because I'm just going through the motions," I exclaimed. "I can't do it anymore. John [my stepdad] was doubly right. When I told him we would come to Cape May for a while this summer and hire someone out here to manage our restaurant, he warned me that anybody we hire won't give it the tender loving care we do. He was talking about our restaurant. What he said, though, also applies to Mom. No nurses we've hired can give her the TLC we can. I want to go back home and take care of her."

Tara's eyes lit up. She held the back of my neck and sang, "We're going home. We're going home."

# *Coming East Again*

They are coming east again, this threesome—No. 2 son, his beloved chosen Native American bride-to-be, and their golden retriever Theo—in a pickup truck they bought at an auction.... I'm already finding myself lying awake nights and they haven't even left California yet.
   —"Joyride" III, June 14, 1995

Back in Santa Cruz after a summer in Cape May, my interests gravitated toward such matters as surfing. One day the phone rang. I picked up the receiver.

"Craig?" inquired the caller.

"Yeah," I responded, not immediately recognizing the voice. "It's John. How's it going?" he said.

I realized it was my stepfather. "Good," I said, "What's up?"

After a brief pause, he continued, "Your mother just had another mild stoke."

It was my turn to pause. "Is she okay?" I asked.

"Well she's at the hospital," he said. "She is in stable condition. The doctor says she is fine, but she's having a lot of trouble moving her right leg."

"That's not fine. That's serious," I exclaimed. "Can I call her? Can she talk?"

"Yes and no," he advised. "She can talk but she is really groggy. Call the house tomorrow and I'll tell you how she is doing. There's one more thing…"

"Yeah?" I said.

"Well, the doctor also did some tests." he continued.

"Yeah, and…" I interrupted.

"She might have Lou Gehrig's disease, but they're not positively sure yet," he remarked.

"What is Lou Gehrig's disease?" I asked. "It's serious, isn't it?"

"It's a neuromuscular disease," he replied. "Its official name is amyotrophic lateral sclerosis."

"Is it fatal?" I asked.

"Yes, but we're not sure she's got it. All this is preliminary right now. Let's just wait and see," he said.

Until then, my mom had ran the household. Now, my stepdad "held down the fort" in Cape May. His employer allowed him to temporarily perform most of his work at home, instead of at his office in Washington, D.C. This was largely possible because my journalist mom already had a fully equipped office in the house. Aside from the income, my stepdad needed to keep his job because his employer's health insurance policy paid most of my mom's hospital, rehab, and medical bills, which were astronomical. Nurses were on duty at the house twenty-four hours a day, seven days a week. The insurance did not pay for them, or for many other costs directly resulting from my mom's illness. Lou Gehrig's is a very expensive disease. It virtually impoverished our family. My stepfather was associate publisher of *The Oil Daily*, a newspaper for the petroleum industry. By the time it was all over, he had resigned and was living off Social Security supplemented by a miniscule freelance writing income.

> It goes without saying that I'm bummed out from what I've been told by the doctors. I can no longer walk and my muscles have become weak. Fatigue is my enemy…. I remember the Gary Cooper movie about Gehrig's life; his standing in a crowded stadium making his farewell to the fans. It always

> broke my heart…. Bad things sometimes do happen to good
> people.
>    —"Joyride" III, August 14, 1996

As my mother's disease worsened, Tara and I closed our small restaurant business in California. It was really too much for us anyway. We made sandwiches at five o'clock in the morning for delivery to wholesale customers, then during the day waited on retail clientele, finally closing the shop at six o'clock each evening. We were barely making ends meet, and probably should have gone out of business sooner. Now we were closing it to return to Cape May, because my mother was dying.

We packed up and drove across the continent. I fantasized that we were going to rescue her. We're going to be her saviors, I thought to myself. We'll make everything right. No longer will mom suffer.

> It was past eleven a.m. when the packing was done. The truck
> looked like something out of *The Grapes of Wrath* when the
> Okies took off for the promised land with all their possessions
> packed inside a rickety truck.
>    —"Joyride" III, June 22, 1995

Unfortunately, this trip turned out to be our time to suffer. Our Mazda B-2000 pickup truck was packed with everything we could think of and then some. Among its contents: two mountain bikes, three surfboards, fifty-two t-shirts, two skateboards, two sleeping bags, one tent, one big-ass 1970-Coleman stove (Tara's grandmother had given it to us three years earlier), three cases of power bars, four five-gallon bottles of water, three flashlights, two twenty-pound bags of California Natural dog food, one golden retriever (male), one sawed off shotgun that Tara's father gave us, one five-gallon Sierra water jar filled to the top with change we'd saved over five years, and one roll of duct tape.

It was the beginning of June. Tara went to the coffee shop around the corner from our house and put up a flyer that read: "Sublet Available June—October. One bedroom with a backyard, a block from the beach." We prepared my son for our long departure. We told him that we'd be gone for the summer and he'd be staying with his mother in Santa Cruz.

We took the Mazda to Rick, our car mechanic. Rick did a little a bit of everything, from working on motorcycles to building decks. He had fiery red hair, wore a grease blackened white T-shirt, and had cuts all over his freckly hands from doing his eclectic jobs. He went over a checklist, shouting orders such as: "Start the engine" and "Turn the headlights on." After a thorough inspection and an oil and filter change, he assured us the truck was ready to go cross country. Tara and I were relieved to hear it was capable of making the trip from Santa Cruz to Cape May. We didn't realize how wrong we were.

> A cross-country trip I took when I was young, we either rented cabins or pitched tents…As No. 2 son, his wife and their faithful frisky dog draw ever nearer, I think of them and the unexpected adventures one comes upon on the open road…
> —"Joyride" III, June 28, 1995

The following morning I called The Hubby and said we were ready to leave and planned to stay in Cape May until October. He seemed happy to hear this, although he sounded weary. I told him the coast-to-coast trip probably would take a week. Hanging up the phone, I turned to Tara and suggested we have as much fun as possible along the way. It turned out to be more of an adventure than outright fun.

# *Big Sur*

We began our drive east by driving south, with our golden retriever hanging his furry head out the back window of our pickup truck's extended cab. Tara suggested we make our first stopover in Big Sur, which is famous for its hot springs and the Esalen Institute. Though the hot springs are open to the public anytime after one o'clock in the morning, we had heard you need to register to use them by five o'clock the previous evening.

Rugged terrain and windy roads with sheer cliffs make driving in Big Sur a little challenging. Getting to the Esalen Institute is even more so. It's strategically placed off the main road and hard to find. Wooden signs at the top of an inclined approach road state: "Visitors are not permitted to drive down. You must walk." So, we parked, turned off our truck's engine, and began walking down the loose gravel-covered road. Our feet slipped downward with every step. After walking about two hundred yards, we came to a guardhouse. Inside was a stern-faced woman. She looked like a female version of Mr. Spock from *Star Trek*. Dressed in tight khaki pants and a multicolored oxford shirt, she poked her head out and asked in a French accent, "Can I help you?" We said we wanted to use the hot tubs that night. She smiled and told us they were closed due to renovation. "They won't open until next year." We glared at her for a few seconds and then walked quietly up the hill toward our truck.

I petted my dog and put the key into the ignition. Nothing happened. Click, click, click, click—nothing. The engine didn't turn over. It was dead. "Craig, did you leave the lights on?" Tara asked.

"No, the lights aren't on," I assured her. "I don't know what's going on."

She reached over my left knee, pulled up the latch to open the hood, stepped out of the truck, and bent down to look at the engine. "All the connections look fine," she said. "Maybe we can push-start it."

Maybe, but not easily. "The only way we can push-start it," I said, "is to go down the road we're not supposed to go down."

We had no choice. After putting the gearshift in neutral, Tara and I pushed the truck on its side and the back. Gravel rolled under our feet. After a few stiff grunts, the truck began rolling. We jumped in and smiled at one another. Our overloaded, oversized white truck with surfboards on top, a dog's head hanging out the side window, and a five-gallon jar full of change—not to mention an illegal firearm—sailed toward the Esalen utopia's little guardhouse.

I popped the clutch into first gear and the engine did nothing. "Again!" Tara yelled. Sweat poured down my forehead and collected in the cleft of my chin. My right knee shook. Mrs. Spock rose from her guardhouse seat as she saw the approaching chariot from hell. Loose dust poured from the back wheels as my dog hung his head out in bliss. "Again, Craig, pop it again, now," demanded Tara. I popped the clutch again. The engine started.

By this time, Mrs. Spock was out of her little guardhouse. Standing erect, as if to block the entrance to the exclusive institute, she raised her right hand as she might have been taught to do during an assertiveness class taught by a nude massager. "Stop!" she screamed in a high-pitched voice. Our pickup truck wasn't about to stop. If we stopped, the engine might stall again. The truck continued descending faster. She suddenly realized we couldn't stop and quickly stepped out of the way. We careened around a bend in the road, sending a cloud of dust toward a picnicking family. It must have been a horrible sight for them, suddenly seeing this vehicle going "where no vehicle has gone before," barreling down on them. As we passed Mrs. Spock, I waved merrily, laughing hysterically.

# Truck Trouble

We became more and more apprehensive about the truck. No way were we going to complete this forty-five-hundred-mile journey without addressing the truck problem. We drove down California Highway 1 as the sun set behind us. Not even a hundred miles away from our Santa Cruz departure point, and already our truck was breaking down. Not that anywhere is a good place to break down, but Big Sur is especially dangerous because there are absolutely no shoulders on the narrow highway.

As the headlights dimmed and the truck began to feel increasingly sluggish, we stopped at the Big Sur Inn. This is a rustic bed and breakfast that sometimes rents rooms for $180 a night. When we got there, only one room was available—for $260. So, Tara and I slept in the truck. Theo was our pillow. Next morning our truck started, stalled, started, stalled, and so on until we made it to the closest town, Carmel. It was raining when we pulled into the parking lot of an auto parts store there. We inquired about an alternator and asked if it was difficult to install. Twenty minutes later, with the help of two auto store employees, we were on our way again, but still paranoid about our truck.

"Ever since we put in the new alternator, this truck hasn't felt right," Tara said as she shifted into fifth gear.

"It didn't feel right when we first drove into Big Sur," I added.

"Yeah, but this is different," she said. "I just have a bad feeling about this."

Always the optimist, I assured her, "You're just freaking out. I'm sure it's fine."

We rarely drove past fifty-five miles per hour for fear we might get stranded again. It was June 14 and we were in the middle of east Texas, where the heat was oppressive. Our truck had no air conditioning. All that seemed to matter was the truck, the heat, and my faraway mother. Hours passed with neither of us speaking a word. We constantly looked at the temperature gauge, hoping it would read "cool." It always seemed to read "hot." We turned the radio on and off, AM to FM, station to station. When we stopped for bathroom breaks, we kept the truck's engine running. When we stopped for water breaks, we kept it running. We were literally petrified to turn the truck off, because it might not start again.

# Jasper, Texas

A local radio station came in clearly, announcing that a sadistic murder had taken place in Jasper, Texas. Someone named James Byrd, Jr. had been beaten and chained and dragged behind a pickup truck until he died. As if our truck was spiritually in tune with the news from the radio broadcast, the little arrow we were watching so attentively had moved from "hot" to "pull-over hot." Tara looked at a map for somewhere to stop. The closest town was Jasper.

"Isn't that where the guy said the murder took place?" I inquired.

"Yeah," she replied.

"Well, we're not pulling over there," I assured her.

"But, we need to pull over because the truck doesn't feel good," she fired back. Our situation was starting to feel like a scene out of a horror movie. Only we weren't caught in the middle of a swamp with some psycho rednecks chasing us. We were in a white Mazda pickup truck driven by a blonde surfer, co-piloted by a beautiful young woman with a golden retriever in the cab, two surfboards on top, and glimmering California license plates.

"We're going to stick out like sore thumbs," I warned.

"We have no choice. We're stopping," she said.

We pulled onto the first exit going into Jasper. To our disbelief, Ku Klux Klan members were staging an armed rally there. Everything in this town was ready to boil over. Shivers went down our spines. Smoke billowed out of our engine. In a way, it seemed symbolic to me that a dark cloud was following us everywhere we went. Now, instead of cruising without a hitch to see my dying mother, we were in a Texas hotspot where a racially motivated killing had just taken place.

We had maps showing the location of KOA campgrounds from Santa Cruz to, yes, Jasper, Texas. Heading toward one, we drove around street corners of the town like we were walking barefoot on nails. Small houses were scattered across wide blocks. We didn't seem to pass anyone unnoticed. I imagined looks showing everything from surprise to sheer hatred among the Jasper residents as they watched our smelly truck appear out of a gray cloud of smut. A KOA was on the outskirts of town. We pulled into the unexpectedly crowded campground and rented a campsite for the night.

From the camp, we called our Santa Cruz mechanic to hear his opinion on what might be wrong with the engine. I dumped a bunch of change from our Sierra water jar and put more than five dollars into a payphone outside the camp's recreation room. Through a screen door I could see a Pac Man video game and a ping-pong table standing on three legs.

"Rick, this is Craig," I hollered into the phone. "You know, your old buddy with the Mazda driving cross country. We're now in Texas and our engine is running really hot and making a pinging sound. You know, like a BB is bouncing around in the engine." Rick asked if it was "a rattling sound." I supposed it was. "Shit, Craig, that's not good," he announced.

Rick said he wanted to hear the noise for himself. Tara slowly drove the truck thirty feet and popped the hood. Then I held the phone receiver over the smoking and rattling engine. Putting it to my ear, I asked Rick, "Well, what do you think?"

He replied, "It doesn't sound good. It sounds like you seized your engine."

"So, what can we do now?" I asked, fully realizing an engine with welded-in pistons is just so much scrap iron.

"Well, Craig," he replied, "I know this will sound strange, but I had a dream that you were towing your truck on a dolly behind a moving truck."

"You're kidding me. You're shitting me. Are you serious?" I asked.

"Yeah, I'm serious," he replied. "Even if that isn't the problem, which I think it is, you're screwed anyway. You don't want some buck-ass mechanic bending you over so you can take it in the pocket."

I knew he probably was right. I wondered out loud how much it would cost to rent and drive a vehicle transport dolly and a moving truck all the way to New Jersey. "A lot of dough," Rick supposed.

"That sucks," I said.

"Give me a call if you figure out it's something else," he replied softly.

"Alright, Rick, thanks a lot," I said. "I appreciate you listening to our engine."

That was it. I was practically in tears. I slammed down the hood and looked at Tara. "We're screwed," I exclaimed.

"What?" she asked.

"Rick said he thinks the engine overheated and now it's seized."

"Really?" she said.

I told her Rick thought we should rent a moving truck with a dolly and tow our truck to Jersey. "Well, what do you think?" she asked, gazing at the truck.

"I think he's right."

> "I'm getting a little old for this," I said to my husband, as I sat on his lap, a suitcase wedged on top of me. The tow truck driver looked at us.
> "You people look familiar," he said.
> "Yeah," I said, "we've been down this road before."
> —"Joyride" III, November 25, 1992

We slept under the Jasper moon that night. Well, Tara did anyway. Upset about so much, including a fear that James Byrd, Jr.'s killers were loose in our vicinity, I remained awake most of the night. Eventually I fell asleep. The following day we rose with the burning Texas sun on our necks. We packed our tent and supplies and went toward town looking for a place to rent a truck. Our first stop was a coffee shop where some young people were outside chatting. We figured that was probably a safe place to stop and ask for directions to truck rental agencies. Tara went inside and asked for a phonebook and two cups of coffee. We sat at an outside table, scanning the yellow pages. Newspapers on some of the tables had headlines that suggested white supremacist fanatics had killed James Byrd, Jr. We found the numbers of a few U-haul dealers and called them for directions. Our truck had barely made it downtown. Now we had to drive three more miles to the rental place, which turned out to be a combination junkyard, vehicle rental outlet, and tire shop.

A young man met us out front. He wore a faded Houston Oilers hat. His jeans were jacked up past his waist. His eyes gazed softly and his hands were filthy with heavy grease.

"How's it going?" I said.

"Fine," he replied.

"We called earlier," I said. "We're having trouble with our truck. We think we should just tow it to where we're going because we have all this stuff packed in it. We're really not sure what is wrong with it."

Eyeing our truck, he asked, "What do you think is wrong with it?"

Tara looked back at it and sighed, "Our mechanic thinks we seized the engine."

"Man, oh, man, that is some hard chicken to swallow," he exclaimed sympathetically. Seeing our rooftop surfboards from afar, he remarked, "You guys seem to be snowboarders. What the hell are you doing in Jasper?"

"Honestly, our mother was just diagnosed with Lou Gehrig's disease," I said. "It's the worst sickness anyone could possibly have. We need to get home and take care of her. We've packed up our whole life, got rid of our business, and got on the road just to have our truck break down."

The young man stepped back, kicked some mud off his shoes, took his hat off, and brushed his dirty fingers through his thick brown hair. After staying silent for a few moments, he said, "I know all about that sick-ass disease. My grandmother died of it."

"I'm sorry," I interrupted.

"You're in for a long haul of heartbreak." Tears went down his nose. "I stayed with her the last six months and fed her baby food. Do you know how it feels to feed baby food to the woman who raised you before she dies? You will and you won't like it at all."

He went on: "A lot of townies think us Texans are slow, but we know a lot more about life itself than the townies know about how much gas mileage they can get out of their Lexus."

Anxious to change the subject, I asked, "So, yeah, you got a moving truck for us with a dolly?"

In fifteen minutes, we were in a twenty-foot U-haul truck with a fifteen-foot dolly attached. We put the $936 cost on our Visa card. After setting our pickup on the dolly, we moved its contents into the U-haul truck. Minutes later, we were heading north out of Jasper.

# The Drive-thru

It took a while to get used to driving a truck-trailer combo. The experience gave us an inkling of what it must be like to handle an eighteen-wheeler. From then on, we would have greater respect for over-the-road teamsters. Singing the words of Billy Joel's *Piano Man*, we shared a bottle of Coke and laughed about our graduation into the realm of real truck drivers.

Being vegetarians, we mostly ate power bars from Costco during our trip, along with bean and cheese burritos from Taco Bell restaurants we stopped at along the way. We had eaten about ten power bars in four hours and they began to taste like cardboard—or maybe that's how they'd always tasted. Tara seemed possessed as she looked for the road sign showing a fork and a plate. This sign often signals a turnoff to fast food restaurants. Suddenly, there it was. Shimmering in all its pseudo-adobe architectural glory, a Taco Bell restaurant.

"Let's do the drive-thru," Tara said.

"Okay, wait, do you think that's a good idea?" I asked, wondering if the drive-thru could accommodate our rig.

"Yeah. No. Maybe. Yeah, it's fine, it'll fit," she assured herself and me.

With no further deliberation, we drove around a bend where an electronic sign portrayed Taco Bell's menu. A pretty voice greeted us in a Texas accent: "Can I help you?" We asked for six bean and cheese burritos and one large Diet Coke. "Please drive around to the window," said the voice. Yep, she said it. "Drive around to the window."

For anyone driving a car, it would be easy. For us, it wasn't that easy. We slowly drove past the glowing electronic sign. With our limited turning radius, we almost smashed into it. As we followed the curve of the cement barrier, instead of turning where we needed to, we decided to make our own route. Our thirty-foot rig wasn't too good at negotiating sharp turns around a fast food drive-thru lane. Suddenly, a horrifying screeching noise came from the back of the dolly. It was like the sound the old fisherman made in the movie *Jaws*, when he scraped his fingernails down a chalkboard.

I screamed, "In God's name: Stop!" Tara threw it into park and I got out and walked around to the back of the truck. To my shock, the axle of the dolly was wedged into the bend of the cement barrier.

You've probably heard those stories about the mother who, following a car wreck, lifted a mini-van to save her three children. Well, that was me, but instead of lifting a mini-van, I pushed from the back of the dolly with all my depleted strength. I screamed and screamed, but the only discernible words were, "Tara, floor it!"

Behind us, cars were backed up and beeping furiously. That chalkboard sound got even louder as the U-haul truck's wheels spun and grabbed for traction. What seemed like hours unfolded in seconds. The axle was grinding against the cement. Suddenly, the wheels dropped to the ground. The truck shook violently and stalled.

A disgruntled manager wearing a neatly tucked-in auburn polo shirt emblazoned with the Taco Bell insignia approached us. "What the hell is going on?" he demanded in a Texas accent.

"We got stuck," Tara explained.

"You're telling me. Look what you've done," he exclaimed. "What do you mean? We haven't done anything. Everything is fine," I insisted.

"You're going have to pay for this damage," he said. "Damage, what damage? There's no damage," I retorted.

"Look at these bushes, they're ruined," he said.

I looked down at the three neatly pruned bushes to which he was referring. Three perfect tire marks now split them into six bushes. I nervously tried to fluff them up.

"They're fine, it's no big deal," I said.

"I'm afraid not; you kids are going to pay for this," he replied, unclipping a cell phone from his brown belt. He removed the fast food headset and dialed a number. My heart sank. I imagined Tara and me sharing a holding cell with the murderers of James Byrd, Jr. He walked about five feet away from us and mumbled into the phone. He then hung up and asked us to pull into the parking lot. Sweat poured down my swollen hands. Tara got into the driver's seat. "I want our six bean and cheese burritos," I told him.

"Okay, that's fine," he replied, motioning to the horrified sixteen-year-old who had watched everything. I got the feeling her innocence was stolen from her that day. What she saw would change her life forever, I thought. She shook nervously as she handed me the bag. Then I demanded my "large Diet Coke." Handing her a ten-dollar bill, I said, "Keep the change!"

Sitting in the truck in the parking lot, we ate as if it was our last meal. Our angst was transferred into the soggy bites of our burritos. We sucked our soda dry, gurgling obnoxiously. Opening up packets of hot sauce, we put them directly into our mouths and squeezed each dry. We pretended to indulge in rebellious and sinful acts. If time had allowed for a conjugal visit, we'd have stripped off our clothes and done it in the middle of the parking lot. However, although no cops had come yet, in my imagination I could hear sirens. Envisioned were two huge Texas state troopers, drawing their automatic weapons and demanding, "Step out of the vehicle!" I considered splitting, but assumed they could catch us on U.S. Route 40. It was a long stretch. It'd be easy to spot us. We weren't exactly inconspicuous.

The manager eyed us from inside the restaurant. Hot sauce dripping from her chin, Tara exclaimed, "Let's get out of here. I can't handle this."

I agreed. "Alright, let's do it," I said. Tara stomped on the pedal. We jetted out of the parking lot. The manager ran after us screaming. In the rearview mirror I saw him stopping after a few yards. Then he threw down his cell phone in disgust.

"Do you think we'll get caught?" I asked.

"Nah, those cops have better things to do than chase after us for some damaged shrubs," Tara assured me.

# *On the Road Again*

We kept driving, stopping only for gasoline and bathroom breaks. We took turns driving and had anxiety attacks whenever we saw state troopers. But we made it through Texas and headed north.

My mother's disease invaded my thoughts second by second. Mile marker after mile marker went by. Sunrises and sunsets rose and fell as we powered toward New Jersey. We arrived in Baltimore, Maryland, about twenty-six hours after leaving the Texas Taco Bell parking lot. It was eight o'clock in the morning. We had hit rush hour. It seemed that whenever something went wrong, it happened at the worst possible moment.

> My bra straps are always falling down. My hem is always unraveling. I get cigarette burn holes in my clothes—and I don't even smoke. If there's an ember within three feet, it's going to find me. If a flock of birds is flying over thousands of miles of space, one of those birds is going to deposit something on me. A single fly in a room will search me out. And land on my nose. If there is a piece of chewing gum within a thousand feet, I bet you I'll sit on it.
> —"Joyride" II, August 22, 1979

# Car Wash

Eventually, I reached a point where I couldn't eat another power bar. Although we're both fervent vegetarians and health food fanatics, when those hypnotic golden arches appeared, we couldn't resist their siren call. Self-control disappeared. We attended long self-discipline classes in our minds. We went through the twelve steps. We admitted we had a problem. But when we saw the glimmering arches, we could resist temptation no longer. "Tara, stop!" I demanded.

"Okay, but no drive-thru this time," she insisted. Tara parked the truck and I ran in and ordered two orange juices and two egg and cheese muffins. I couldn't wait to tear into our glorious junk food sandwiches. Those white-flour doughy pieces of joy. And the egg; yes, the egg was real egg, although at that point I probably wouldn't have cared if it was freeze-dried egg, like the astronauts eat.

Upon leaving the McDonald's parking lot, we drove into the lot of an adjacent car wash. It seemed to offer enough room to completely turn around. As we drove in long sweeping arcs, our U-haul truck's trailer hitch began to encounter severe stress and strain. The lot was on an extremely steep incline. As we backed up, the trailer dolly went left as we went right. The more left we went, the more right the dolly went. Soon we were stuck, so stuck the hitch was almost ready to break off.

Tara and I finally cracked. After more than two hours in the car wash lot, we still hadn't turned our truck-trailer combo. The hitch scraped on the incline every time we tried something new. Both of us became snippy. "You try it, genius," Tara snapped. "You're the one who decided to stop at McDonald's, and you're the one who decided to turn around in this fucking car wash—you fucking idiot."

"Oh yeah, well, you're the one who decided to go through the drive thru at Taco Bell," I retorted. "That was a brilliant fucking maneuver. Yeah, let's decide to drive through the Taco Bell with a twenty-foot moving van and a fifteen-foot dolly. What kind of shit is that?" I griped.

We were flipping out. We considered strangling one another right there in the abandoned parking lot. It was easy to envision some crusty old veteran police officer and rookie trainee coming across our dead bodies, our hands still gripped around each other's necks. Rather than around my neck, Tara placed her hands on the steering wheel and, in a brilliant moment of determination, drove the truck-trailer directly toward the car wash facility. Instead of trying to turn around, she drove almost straight ahead. Like a sewer threading a needle, she guided the truck-trailer through a narrow corridor designed to house the big wash brushes and blowers.

Suddenly, the clouds moved. The skyline shifted. A streak of light broke out of the gray and shone down on our truck-trailer. I shrieked as she narrowly missed the roof of the car wash. But she did it. We were on our way again.

As we headed toward Cape May, our nerves remained frayed. We even contemplated getting a divorce. It was over, I said to myself. She was going back to Santa Cruz right after we unloaded in Cape May.

> He gets it from his mother....
> As we rolled through Ohio, the women started arguing and it got worse as we invaded the Iowa cornfields. By the time we got to the Badlands, I had a migraine headache that didn't go

away. The two women fought over road signs and which restaurant to eat in.

By this time my companion was beginning to get on my nerves. We had been traveling for ten days, with very little in common except we had both been told to get out of a car in Cheyenne, Wyoming.

Eventually we made our way to California…

—"Joyride" III, October 14, 1992

# *Jefferson Street*

Nine days and two hours after leaving Santa Cruz, we arrived in Cape May. As we approached the front door at 314 Jefferson Street, all thoughts of divorce vanished. People we had never seen before were walking in and out. I felt like an old dog coming back to his old stomping grounds, hoping to reclaim the territory that once was his sole domain, only to find other dogs comfortably situated there. Gazing at all the new folks, I inched into the doorway. A small brown-skinned nurse with beautiful round cheeks greeted me at the door. She spoke exquisitely, with an African accent, "Hello, you must be No. 2." I smiled and looked over her shoulder, toward the middle of the living room, hoping to see my sick mother. All I saw was an empty hospital bed.

"Uh, what's your name?" I asked.

"Jebba," she said proudly. "And this must be your beautiful Californian wife, who surfs too."

"Yep," Tara replied.

"Come in and sit down," she said.

"Where is she?" I asked.

"She is in the bathroom; do not disturb," she insisted. "I'll be right back," I told Tara, leaving her with Jebba. I walked out the same front door I had entered so eagerly five minutes earlier. Turning away from the street, I walked down the driveway and swung open the large, creaky door of the garage. The garage was littered with superficial things my mom could no longer use: a wheelbarrow, a couple of shovels, a lawnmower, a ladder, etc. I hopped over the cluttered floor and reached for my trusty beach cruiser. In a moment, that old bike was between my legs, moving toward the oceanfront as fast as I could peddle it. Reaching the seawall, which protects the expensive houses along Beach Drive, I used the bicycle's seat as a step-up ladder to jump to its top. Before me lay my favorite beach, where my mom took me when I was a little boy.

There were no waves. I snapped back to reality. On return to my mom's house, I skidded into the driveway, leaned the bike against the brick steps, and hurriedly entered. My mom had returned to her living-room bed. Tara was propping her pillow and discussing ways to make her feel more comfortable. A wave of depression came over me. My mom's bottom half was covered by a blue sheet. Her curly hair, once dark black, was riddled with thick gray waves. I hugged and kissed her, then started to cry. Wiping the tears away, I reminded myself that for her sake I should be calm and composed.

"Craig, you and Tara made it," my mom said, smiling. "Did you bring the dog?"

Tara replied, "Yes, but Jebba won't let him in because she's worried about his hair."

"His hair? Oh, he'll be fine," my mother assured us.

"You don't need to be breathin' in all that dog hair," advised Jebba. "He's sheddin' and it's probably not good for you to breathe that stuff in."

Tara believed Jebba was probably right. "I'm sure she knows best," said Tara assuredly.

"He'd be good for me; bring that big boy in," my mom said. "Not right now, mom," I replied.

"I said, bring that big boy in," she insisted. It was reassuring to hear her speak that way. She sounded then like the take-no-nonsense-from-Craigie-mom of my boyhood.

"Okay," I agreed, hesitantly. Exiting the living room, I opened the screen door and called, "Theo!"

Barreling in recklessly, our big golden retriever knocked over a glass of water, which spilled into my mother's lap. Theo spun around twice and flopped down in the middle of the floor. "You see; that wasn't so bad, he just wanted to come in," she smiled.

"Mom I'm sorry about the spill. Let me get a towel," I said. Before I could make a move in that direction, Tara immediately walked toward the kitchen to retrieve one. As they passed one another in the hallway, Jebba asked, "What's going on?"

I heard her question and replied, "Oh, nothing. Theo spilled some water on Libby's lap."

Again, the characteristic protectiveness of the nursing profession surfaced: "That's not nothing. I told you two that I didn't want that dog in here," she snapped. To me this was a home. To the nurses, this was more like a hospital.

"Don't worry about the dog. We'll take care of him," Tara assured everyone.

# Old House, New Surroundings

The caregivers and frequent visitors watched my mother's disease slowly progress. Less frequent visitors usually were shocked by the change they noticed from the previous time they had seen her. It was shocking to see the toll the disease had taken during my absence. I stared at her paralyzed legs and lifeless, outwardly-pointing feet. To relieve my anxiety, I dropped to the living room floor and began to do pushups. "What are you doing?" my mom asked.

"Keeping in shape," I replied.

Her voice sounding slightly slurred, she declared, "You're wasting all your energy. You could be using it to run downtown and get me a cheese steak."

By that time, the disease was affecting her vocal chords, but obviously not her appetite nor sense of humor.

I chuckled and stopped my pushups. "Mom, you can't have a cheese steak. That stuff is bad for you," I said.

"I'm going to die anyway. What does it matter?" she replied. "Mom, don't talk like that," I said.

"Don't talk like what?" she asked.

"Like you're going to die," I replied.

"I am, Craig. Face it, I am going to die. You know it, and I know it."

Rising from the floor, I walked to her bed and puffed her pillow. Tears were streaming down her face. Grabbing a tissue from the table next to the bed, I wiped her nose. "Mom, please don't talk like this. Ok, I'll get the cheese steak. You want fried onions? You want ketchup? How about honey mustard? You want some Swiss on it? How about your roll?"

"My roll?" she asked.

"Yeah, your roll," I said. "You want your roll toasted, semi-toasted, or do you want it crusty, the way it comes freshly baked out of the oven?"

She seemed puzzled. "Does it matter? Just get me something good," she said. Then we both laughed.

# Lou Gehrig's Disease 101

Doctors, nurses, visitors, workmen, and delivery people offered suggestions on how to help my mom be more comfortable. Even *she* did. She'd tell me to move a pillow to a particular location, to fluff it a certain way, how to rearrange a blanket, etc. No matter what we did, however, it's my opinion that after Lou Gehrig's disease struck her down, she never was truly comfortable. This malady slowly destroyed every bodily function that we take for granted. If an insect landed on her, she couldn't swish it away. If she itched, she couldn't scratch. Unlike most of us, if she felt uncomfortable sitting or lying in a certain position, she couldn't simply roll over. Someone else had to adjust her body. If it wasn't done properly, she was miserable. Not surprisingly, it's difficult to adjust someone's body to their own liking. Your body is your body. No one really understands what feels just right to you except you. I learned quickly that when she would ask me to help her "feel more comfortable," the proper response was more complicated than rocket science. Almost like a domino effect, when you moved a part of her body, say a leg, another part, such as an arm, would need adjusting. If I moved her pillow, her shoulder would stick to the bed. If I moved her blanket, her back would become lodged in the crease of the bed. To get everything just right sometimes took an hour or more. I'd silently cuss at myself whenever she seemed unhappy with my "comfort" efforts.

As Cape May was usually a very quiet town, her groaning echoed throughout the house at night. Even at two or three or four in the morning, when we'd hear her moan or call, we'd rush to her bedside. Even when she was silent, we'd periodically check on her.

For several weeks, Tara and I took turns as night nurses, to help save money for the family. When we began, we never realized what the job would entail. "I'm going to be like the nurses on the *St. Elsewhere* and *ER* television shows," I told myself. As it turned out, it wasn't like on the TV dramas. It was a very demanding and often heart-wrenching job. For one thing, the night nurse never slept. It wasn't uncommon for either one of us to periodically get drowsy during the daytime. Sometimes I drank five cups of coffee and a couple of shots of ginseng just to keep my lids up. Unlike on the TV doctor and nurse shows, care-giving is emotionally draining. For instance, seeing Tara wipe my mom's bottom was really distressing to me. My mom felt uncomfortable having her do it, but there was no choice. I know I didn't want to do it, and was grateful Tara took that burden from me. Tara did it willingly and seemed to fit right into the role of caregiver. When she was very young, her mother worked as a schoolteacher, and Tara dressed and fed her younger sister and brother. Although Tara had known Libby for only two years, they quickly became close friends. Now, don't get me wrong: Even for someone with care-giving experience, caring for a Lou Gehrig's disease victim is incredibly difficult. From time to time, Tara freaked out. Some nights we hugged one another for hours. I recall one night she said she could "hardly think straight" because the situation seemed so overwhelming.

# *Beach Patrol*

Cape May was hot and muggy that summer. The humidity index hit a whopping ninety-six percent. An occasional cooling southeast wind blew in from the ocean, as it did at about three o'clock one afternoon. At that time, Tara was attending Beach Patrol Rookie School. She'd applied for lifeguard duty after hearing me talk about my adventures as an ocean lifeguard. From a young age, Tara had swum competitively in pools and was anxious to join the beach patrol. In the tryout, she swam and ran faster than most of the guys. She endured a good deal of taunting, as some guards evaluated her bust more than her swimming stroke. She was a freaking demon possessed. No matter how much they tried to break her, she kept smiling. Her days were filled with five-mile runs in the soft hot sand, and then a two-mile swim against the current in the ocean. Every night she came home with blisters on her feet and hives all over her body. She was having an allergic reaction to something. Every time she started her long runs, she'd get hives the size of small fists all over her body.

Come nighttime, I had one hand rubbing my mom's feet to increase her circulation, and the other icing Tara's back. Tara told stories of agonizing beach workouts. Sitting up against her pillow, Mom would occasionally proclaim, "I could do that. That doesn't sound so hard." My mother was never athletic. She facetiously boasted that she was the first woman to surf the big waves of Hawaii. Although she had taken a trip to the Hawaiian islands of Maui and Oahu once, and had made several trips to California, she'd never surfed anywhere. In reality, my mom's main exercise had been riding her three-wheel bike around Cape May island.

That year, the media-hyped El Niño helped generate fierce waves and erratic weather patterns. One day it would rain; the next day would be sunny. At times, the wind blew north at speeds up to twenty-five mph for three days, producing terrific waves. Fortunately, I had been given a key to the paddleboard storage area at Beach Patrol Headquarters to train in the early mornings on a twelve-foot paddleboard. Every day, I was out in the water by six-thirty a.m., headed either east or west. I counted every stroke by twos, usually reaching thirty thousand, then counted back down again. Some days the ocean was like a sheet of glass, and my strokes became methodical; I imagined myself as a Buddhist monk walking for miles up winding paths to a mountaintop temple. Every so often, bottlenose dolphins would swim alongside me. I called them my silent partners, because they did not utter a sound.

# *Voodoo*

Medical professionals came and went to and from my mom's house. The agency that provided nurses preferred immigrants from Africa. Nurses from Liberia, Ghana, and Nigeria—and a few from varied Caribbean islands—would stay for a few days or a few weeks. Two particularly professional ones stayed for many months. Ever the joker, I'd ask any nurse who was dark-skinned and female, "Do you know voodoo?" Usually this brought an incredulous stare. They'd snap back an answer such as: "Do you think all people from Africa know voodoo, young man?" Or, "Yes I know voodoo. Do you need some voodoo done?" Eventually, it became a family joke that Craig would conduct an interview of each new nurse as follows: "Have you been a nurse a long time? Do you have experience with this type of patient? What hours do you prefer? Do you know voodoo?"

Medical equipment and supply trucks arrived almost daily. Items came and departed through the front doors, back door, and side door. As my mom's illness worsened, new pieces of equipment would replace their predecessors. Wheelchairs came and went. Mattresses were exchanged. When a bed lift mechanism broke, they wouldn't replace it; they'd deliver a new bed. There were substitute oxygen tanks, hydraulic lifts, and mechanical, electrical, and electronic instruments and apparatuses. Sweaty, barrel-chested men tromped in and out, oblivious to my mom's pain and suffering. "Hush!" a nurse would say, as my mother lay soundly asleep maybe for the first time in forty-eight hours. "Stop that clumsy banging!" Mostly, the deliverymen showed total disinterest in her condition, whether we knew how to use the equipment, or if we could afford to pay for the stuff. "Just sign here," they'd say in a Jersey or Philly accent. They didn't seem to care if anything worked or not.

# *The Good Old Days*

A new wheelchair appeared at the front door. The wheels resembled mountain bike tires, or a very small version of monster-truck tires. "Mom, can I borrow this," I asked jokingly.

"Borrow what?" she asked.

"Your new wheelchair," I said smirking.

"What are you going to do with it?" she asked.

"Jump things," I replied. "You know, dirt mounds. Go off the seawall. I think the kid down the street has a skateboard ramp."

She looked pensive. "You do what you want with it. Soon, I won't need it anymore," she said.

"Stop that!" I demanded.

"Stop what?" she asked.

"That," I said firmly.

"What?" she asked again.

"The 'I won't need this and that.' Why can't you joke with me?" I remarked.

"Because I'm being honest, Craig. You need to understand my condition and what's coming."

I didn't want to be serious. I wanted to make light of the situation. Frankly, I needed to joke around. I needed a laugh. Maybe she didn't. I did. Is that so bad? Maybe because of the column, I've always had a sense of humor. I grew up listening to Steve Martin's *King Tut* song and Bill Cosby's *Noah and the Ark* routine. Whenever I was sad or indifferent, I went up to my room and listened to those guys. My mom loved to laugh, too.

This time my mom was crying. Jebba came from the kitchen and heard mom sobbing. She wore a white in-house nurse dress, white shoes, and black socks. She entered a room with authority and questioned everybody and everything. "What is going on? What are you doing to your sweet mother?" she asked.

"What do you mean, what am I doing?" I said. "I'm not doing anything. We're talking. I'm joking. You're butting in."

Jebba looked sympathetically at my mom and said, "Libby is crying. That's no good. She will choke on all that mucus she has from you joking or whatever you're doing."

She grabbed a tissue, gently squeezed mom's nose, and told her to blow. Mom blew and blew and blew. Jebba wiped the tears from her eyes and fluffed her pillow. She looked at her watch and announced, "It is time for Libby's nap. She needs rest."

Especially on the first floor, the house had a hospital feel to it. The nurses would complain that I was tracking beach sand into the house. In the laundry room, the washing machine and dryer seemed to be always running. Someone was in the kitchen constantly, boiling water, putting medicine into the refrigerator, cleaning, or talking on the telephone.

I wanted the old days back, when I could track sand into the house without guilt. I wanted things the way they once were, when my mom and I sat on the front porch watching the tourists parking their cars and unloading their folding chairs, beach toys, and inflatable rafts. We would sit there chuckling at the stuff they felt they needed to enjoy a day on the beach.

> Going to the beach, the children hop along, proudly carry their buckets and shovels; a few hours later they are tired and cranky, refusing to carry gear, and crying to be carried.
> —"Joyride" III, July 6, 1994

Sitting on the porch is better than going to the movies. The show is funny and—well—it's free.

Here comes a young family. They ought to hire a moving van. They're lugging beach umbrellas, towels, sand chairs, lounge chairs, a picnic hamper, and tote bags filled with books and toys. (I'll bet they won't get much reading in this trip).

Here comes older couple. I'd have trouble identifying them because they're swathed in huge beach towels, their faces nearly covered with umbrella-sized straw hats and No. 15+ sun block. Their eyes are shielded with sunglasses, and their noses are covered with little plastic devices to keep the sun off. If I didn't know better, I'd think they were from Mars or some other alien planet.

Here comes a teenage couple; from afar they look like one person as they come walking along with their arms around one another. I guess I'm jealous a little bit of how the girl is wearing that bikini—and her sweet youth. Oh, well.

Now I see a couple of boys, walking well ahead of their mom and dad. Yuck, parents. They are pushing and shoving one another, and gosh, they're funny to watch, reminding me, I guess, of No. 1 and No. 2 sons a long time ago.

—"Joyride" III, July 6, 1994

I remember one time when I chuckled so much that I spilled watermelon juice all over my crotch. I knew those days were gone and I was pissed.

What had been the dining room now held hospital equipment that wasn't needed anymore or that would be needed in the future. The hoist was in there. It looked like one of those mini-cranes. It had a big crank and long black nylon straps so Mom could sit in there and be lifted out of bed and put into her wheelchair. There were hospital tray tables that no longer worked because I'd either broken them while setting them up or they were too small for all the water and medicine she needed. On one side of the room was a fold-out couch, so the on-duty nurse would have a place to rest. The din-

ing room table and chairs had long since been moved to the second
floor.

# *A Night Out*

One night Tara and I went out for a few beers. My brother, Keith, No. 1, in town for the weekend, stayed with Mom. When we got to the bar, it was packed. Every lifeguard we worked with was there, having a merry time.

> Some men in their lives want to hit balls that are remembered in legendary world series; some men want to fly planes that cross continents or vast oceans.
>
> But there are others who are driven to dream of sitting atop lifeguard stands, to be remembered not for where they stood, but for where they sat.
>
> I approach the stand with a sense of wonder. That's my kid up there, I tell myself.
>
> A man among men. A man among women. A man little kids are awed by. A man that parents entrust with their babes in arms. A man that old men will watch, remembering when they, too, had their moment in the sun.
>
> —"Joyride" III, July 26, 1989

Suddenly, a DJ announced: "Whichever side of the bar sings the loudest will get twenty-five cent drinks for the next fifteen minutes." Coerced to one side of the bar by friends, we sang along, skipping every word until the chorus "Sweet Caroline, Oh, Oh, Oh. Good Times Never Seemed So Good" came along. Our side won, and Tara and I were downing as many twenty-five-cent drinks as we could, when out of the shadows came Chuck, an old acquaintance. Though he'd formerly sported a boot camp haircut, he now had a flowing mane that made him resemble the Jesus Christ of medieval paintings. "Well, holy shit," he said. "Look who it is: Craig and Tara." He said he was only in town for a couple of days and was returning the next day to Hollywood, Florida, where he worked as a full-time lifeguard. After telling him we were now Californians but in Cape May for the summer, he asked if he could crash on our living room sofa before leaving for Florida. "Sure," I said, not giving a second thought to the fact that at my place, the living room was my mom's hospital-like bedroom.

As Chuck staggered off, Tara exclaimed, "He can't stay over, you idiot." Realizing she was right, I thought to myself that he'd probably forget he even spoke with us, or if he did, he wouldn't remember where we lived. Near last call, as we edged toward the back door, Chuck came out of a crowd of girls and hollered, "Yo dude. Gimme a piggy back," and jumped atop my shoulders. "Take me to your humble abode. Giddy-up, boy." Pulling him down to a standing position, I put my arm around him and began to walk him home. He fell into a drunken stupor hanging on my shoulder.

Chuck could fall asleep anywhere. I mean anywhere. He once bragged about falling asleep after a party and waking up cuddling with a skunk. "Yeah man, I was spooning that skunk," he said. "Hell, that skunk was stoked to have me to keep it all warm."

We walked the seven blocks from the bar to my mom's house, taking turns half-carrying, half-dragging Chuck. We pulled him up the brick steps and into the house, quietly placing him on the sofabed in the dining room. Meanwhile, No. 1 son and Mom were asleep in the living room. Jebba, the nurse, was asleep upstairs. Chuck will be fine, I thought. I'll have him out by early morning. Then, Tara and I went upstairs and fell asleep.

In the middle of the night, I heard a high-pitched scream. I jumped out of bed and leaped downstairs. It was Jebba, alarmed and scared. Was Mom in trouble? The screaming came from the combination mini-bathroom/laundry room. I ran there and saw Jebba, still screaming, standing outside the room's doorway.

"What the hell is going on?" I demanded. Looking over her shoulder, I saw Chuck, completely naked, laying on the little floor with his legs and arms spread out. Jebba was chanting hysterically, "Jesus…oh Jesus…oh Jesus."

Turning to her, I quipped, "No, not Jesus; it's Chuck. He just looks like him."

No longer visibly upset, she now seemed merely tired and bewildered. "Huh?" she said.

"Yeah, that's my friend Chuck," I assured her. "It's fine, really. Go back to bed. I'll take care of this."

I pushed Jebba out of the room and grabbed Chuck under his shoulders. He had fallen asleep while trying to use the toilet. No. 1 and Mom had slept soundly through the whole incident, which, as far as I was concerned, was best for everyone.

# Harry Houdini and Tom Sawyer

From time to time, I would pull a Harry Houdini act to escape the hospital-like atmosphere when it became overbearing. I'd just leave and not tell anyone where I was going. I'd escape to a more carefree environment, with friends who were uninvolved and largely unconcerned with my mom's illness or any of my other problems. With them, life mostly was fun. People in the house would wonder where I went.

Shawn, Chuck's brother, was a loud young Cape May lifeguard who loved to exercise. He and I paddled together. A former scholarship swimmer from the University of Delaware, he broke his shoulder midway through his junior year and had to stop competing in swim meets. He still could swim fast, but not fast enough for competition racing. Paddling didn't seem to bother him. He was a sprinter, and super-fast in almost any physical activity. He could sprint fifty yards faster than anyone else on the beach patrol. As we paddled together, the paddling got longer. Instead of four miles, we went seven. He did back flips down the beach. He sang cheesy 1980s songs as we paddled: "I have a pi-ct-ure pinned to my wall. An image of you and of me and we're laughing. We're loving it all. Whoaaaaa, Whoaaaa, Whoaaa. Hold me now, Ohhhhhh warm my heart…." <u>Thompson Twins</u>. Hold Me Now. Released 01 July 1984. Cassette. Arista. Thompson Twins, Tears for Fears, Madonna, and Simple Minds were some of his favorites. Shawn was the youngest of three brothers. His dad was nicknamed "Fish" by the family for some unknown reason. Shawn was my friend and confidant. During my Houdini-act runaways, he was Tom Sawyer and I was Huck Finn.

# *General Hubby*

The Hubby ran the household and nursing operation like a general in the army. He handled the bills that flooded in, catching overcharges and double billings. He reviewed all invoices and delivery slips. If he found an error, he would call both the provider and the insurance company. He discovered, for instance, that an ambulance company that transported my mother to and from a Philadelphia hospital later fraudulently billed, and was paid for, transporting her to and from hospitals to which she never had gone.

A friend of my mom's, a retired accountant named Judy, came on Mondays to help The Hubby with the paperwork. Afterward, she'd spend maybe five or ten minutes visiting Mom. She complained constantly about the tourists taking up parking spaces in front of her house.

She fidgeted and twirled her index fingers while conversing, looking aimlessly out the windows or staring at our cluttered mantle, which held a slew of family pictures capturing Forrest family moments: graduations, baby shots, family portraits, and first-day-of-school photos. Judy belonged to the local tennis club. Her home was in Bethesda, Maryland, and she came to Cape May for holidays and weekends. Though she came to our house to help, it always seemed to me that from the minute she arrived she wanted to leave. Influential and important Cape May businessmen, politicos, and socialites attended cocktail parties at her house. She often came wearing her tennis outfit, making me wonder how insensitive she must be to remind my mother how she could not move a muscle.

Every time Judy came, I wanted to leave and go to my extended family, the nonchalant Beach Patrol guys for whom life was rarely solemn.

# *Books on Tape*

Recently I've discovered audio books. As my illness has progressed, my hands have become impaired, making it difficult to turn the pages of a book…. Listening to an audio book is a little like going to a theater where I am the only one in the audience.
  —"Joyride" III, March 12, 1997

My mom occasionally escaped. She seemed to fall into a trance when she listened to her books on tape. I'd scour the public library looking for books that might interest her. Some were boring, some entertaining. Important to her was the voice of the person narrating. Although her hands could no longer hold a book, her mind could hold a story. I brought home John Grisham novels that dealt with intrigue and corporate scandals. She seemed bored by some bestsellers, so I began bringing books on gardening, carpentry, and electrical work. She thought this was a joke at first, but I told her it was for real. She laughed and said, "Maybe I can learn a new trade."

After hours of adjusting my mom's limp body, rearranging pillows, handling bedpans, providing glasses of water, etc., I'd prepare to leave the house at six in the morning. One of the day nurses would come and take over. Tara and I took turns staying up. That way we each got an adequate amount of sleep, because lifeguards can't risk falling asleep on the job. Still, when I left the house each morning, I was exhausted, more mentally than physically.

# Paddle Around the Island

In addition to my friend Shawn, my Tom Sawyer, I became close friends with an older guard named Dan. He loved to fish and surf. He had two webbed toes. At parties, he would display them (after the partygoers had a slightly smooth buzz going). Girls would circle around his right foot and go, "Oooh" and "Ahhh." Rumor had it that his great grandfather played on the same U.S. water polo team as the Great Duke, the Hawaiian Prince who brought surfing to America. Dan worked all winter as a construction journeyman. He timed his jobs so that they ended in time to be a lifeguard during the summer. The youngest of thirteen brothers and sisters, he was tall, athletic, and rugged looking. Girls found him attractive. That he loved being a lifeguard was apparent in the way he lived his life.

"Let's paddle around the Cape May Island," Dan suggested one morning. My eyes lit up. I was immediately ignited. We checked the tide chart and determined that a week from that Saturday was the best time. We hoped to paddle against the tide for about two miles and supposed we might be able to swing around on the oncoming high tide. The circumference of the island was exactly 11.3 miles. A constant southeast wind blew early in the day. This made any ocean journey difficult.

The crack of dawn was the time we set to embark on the island paddle. Big, bright houses stretched along the beachfront. Pink, blue, purple, and yellow, these bed-and-breakfast houses were scattered everywhere. Motorboats buzzed past. Tourists and fishermen on day charters waved. Our dolphin friends occasionally followed us.

We stopped for water and power-bar breaks and kept heading east. We entered the canal and stayed to the right, out of harm's way. Monstrous boats with fish and gear sailed past. Boat captains normally do not look out for paddle boarders, especially in the canal. We stayed even with one another.

I often daydream when I paddle for a long time. My arms move constantly, but I'm not aware of the motion. I can go hours and miles and forget or remember everything.

> The other day I came across an article supporting the view that daydreaming is okay. According to the article, daydreaming helps us to get our act together and offers relief from everyday pressures.
>
> Now knowing that the experts consider daydreaming okay has given me a different view of things. For instance, yesterday when No. 2 came around looking for something to do, I suggested he go away and daydream.
> —"Joyride" II, April 19, 1978

While paddling, I recalled how my brother and I went into business together as kids. He'd lend me ten dollars to buy Dixie cups, sugar, and lemonade mix. We then placed a cooler chest into my trusty rusty wagon. I pulled it up and down the boardwalk, pouring the lemonade into cups and offering it for sale. Acting as both mentor and security guard, my brother sat on nearby benches and observed. "I got ice-cold lemonade here, only twenty-five cents," I'd shout. Sometimes we came home with twenty-five dollars in loose coins. That's not bad for a nine-year-old peddler. Needless to say, when it came time to repay my brother the initial ten-dollar investment, I complained.

Back to reality: We paddled under two ninety-foot suspension bridges that span the Cape May canal. Rust and corrosion were evident on the towering support beams. Birds hid beneath the bridges, in crevices along steel platforms. Bird droppings littered the area and there was a strong stench of rotting fish. It was noon and the temperature was ninety degrees. In the canal, there was no breeze. However, as we exited the canal a stiff onshore wind cooled our faces. There was texture on the ocean, and the wind was blowing at twenty-five knots. Only halfway to our destination, it was already three o'clock. We needed to get moving.

We tried to hug the beach so the current wouldn't drag us out to sea. Currents around the point where Delaware Bay meets the Atlantic Ocean are infamous. They have caused many weary boaters and swimmers great harm. As we paddled harder, we seemed to be getting nowhere. Ocean spray shot into our noses and mouths, making every breath wet and salty. There was nothing we could do other than keep our heads down and stroke. We drafted off one another and took turns leading and making a wake. As paddlers, each of us had our strong points. Dan was the biggest and strongest. Shawn was fast. I had endurance.

Three miles to go and high tide was in full rush. Every three strokes brought us only about half a stroke forward. It was five o'clock, and we had been in the water for eight hours. We were getting tired. Shawn would fall back and Dan and I would wait; then Dan would start to fall back, and then me. The going was slow. If we stopped to rest, we would drift backwards. About a half-mile later, around six o'clock, Tara paddled up in an ocean kayak. (I had told her we planned to paddle the island.) "You guys have been gone all day. I've been worried," she said.

The four of us passed by a half-sunken cement ship, which had been there since sometime shortly after World War I. It later became a tourist attraction. To us, it was just another marker along our journey. The time had come. With the wind in our faces blowing harder than ever, we headed in, riding the windy waves. When we hit the beach, we saw hundreds of spectators who had come to watch the South Jersey Lifeguard Competition being held that day. With a salty taste in my mouth, as my toes sunk into the wet sand, I felt dizzy but happy—really happy. Dan displayed a huge grin. Shawn ran up the beach to catch the swim event. I hugged Tara and whispered to her, "I'm going to paddle from Delaware to here, for Mom."

She brushed off my remark, and we walked toward the event. The next day I mentioned the idea of a paddle from the other side of the bay separating the state of Delaware and Cape May County to Shawn and Dan. They liked the idea but warned that it could be very difficult. Peak tides there can sometimes throw large oil tankers off course. Also, Delaware Bay is a breeding ground for sharks. I figured if we left from Cape Henlopen, Delaware, and trekked due northeast back to Cape May, the journey would be seventeen point eight miles.

For me, paddling from Delaware seemed easy compared to the difficulty of watching mom's illness progressively worsen. Her physical appearance changed every day. Her hands were now thin and bony. Her face had atrophied and her cheeks began to look baggy. Her feet never moved. Only her left hand was mobile.

# Brotherly Differences

No. 1 son, when he was growing up, claimed he was a winter man, liking cold and wind.

No. 2 son—a born summer man if ever there was—found winter a temporary nuisance that fell between late summer and early spring.

—"Joyride" III, November 15, 1995

On weekends, No. 1 and his wife sometimes came down to Cape May from their Philadelphia home. I knew her before my brother did. She and I met while I was bartending in Santa Cruz, California, where she was visiting friends. Her home was then in Erie, Pennsylvania. "You live in Erie? My brother lives in Erie. He looks like Tom Cruise," I said. (I lied.) She seemed intrigued, so I gave her No. 1's phone number. After she returned to Erie, she called him and invited him to lunch. "It was love at first lunch," my brother tells people. A year later my brother told me he was getting married and asked me to be the best man. This wasn't a big deal. No. 1 wasn't best man at my wedding.

Tara stayed behind and ran the shop while I traveled to Erie for my big brother's wedding. After driving to the San Francisco airport, I flew from there to Cleveland, Ohio. From there, I took a two-hour taxi ride to Erie. I wasn't prepared for the freezing weather. Cleveland in October was colder than Santa Cruz on its coldest winter day. The taxi driver wore earmuffs and talked about how he was saving his money to go to the Bahamas for a week to frolic in the warm Caribbean sun. I told him I was a surfer. "A surfer in Cleveland? What are you doing here?" he asked.

"My brother is getting married," I said.

"No kidding; you won't have any fun here. This place sucks," he shared.

> Erie is twelve hours away as the crow flies. Twelve long hours traversing Jersey. Then up, up, up and away to the northern-most corner of Pennsylvania. It sits on (where else?) Lake Erie. Bring your snuggies, as my mother used to say.
> —"Joyride" III, May 31, 1995

My brother's wedding took place in the courtyard of a Victorian-style hotel. Mom couldn't be there because at that time, she was post-stroke, bedridden, and experiencing the early stages of Lou Gehrig's disease. Keith sent me a Robert Frost poem a week before I flew out and told me he wanted the best man to recite it. Two hours before the wedding, No. 1 came to my room. Looking down at the flip-flops on my feet, he surprised me with the news that he had decided to ask an old friend of his to be his best man. I was stunned. "You remember Tony?" he said.

"Yeah, I guess so," I replied.

"Well, he came all the way out from New York and..."

"Well, I came all the way from California," I quickly interjected.

"Yeah you're right, but you're my brother," he continued. "So?" I snapped back.

"So, I think it's better if he's the best man," he declared. "So, you don't want me to read the Robert Frost poem?" I mused.

"No, he will," said No. 1. "I'd just appreciate it if you would say a few words. You know, about how she and I met—that type of stuff."

"Okay," I sighed, still reeling from the surprise.

After he sauntered out of the room, I stared out the hotel room window, realizing I had been demoted from starting pitcher to bench warmer before the umpire even had a chance to holler, "Play ball!"

I had been reduced from best man to "saying a few words." Yeah, I'll say a few words, I thought. I'll say, "You stupid ungrateful moron, how could you do this to me?" I'll say, "I'm sorry I ever introduced the two of you." Taking out a pen and notebook, I began to write appropriate missives. I scribbled scathing insults and horrible profanities, then began writing a note to our mother, telling her how disgusted I was with my hypocrite brother.

Then I cowardly crumpled my writings, threw them away, and walked downstairs looking for as many free beers as I could find. "Yeah, I'm going to get drunk, really drunk, and make a complete fool of myself and of my brother," I told myself. "I'll strip naked, scream 'tyranny,' grab Keith's insidious top hat, and do a rowdy song and dance routine, maybe from *Annie Get Your Gun* or *Little Shop of Horrors*."

Actually, when asked to speak, I stepped to the podium and politely but majestically said, "Mom would've liked to have been here for my brother's wedding. If she could, she'd have walked here all the way from Cape May. And while she's not here in person, she wants you to know she's here in spirit, and sends her blessings and good wishes to you all." That was it. No stinging barbs. No nude dance routine. Everyone clapped. Mom's Hubby cried. Tony read the Robert Frost poem. People at the marriage ceremony and the party following all seemed to be happy and enjoying themselves. Not me, however. I felt very sad, not because my brother dumped me as best man, but because Mom wasn't here, because she was suffering so terribly, and because I knew that at that moment she wanted to be there so very much.

Three days after No. 1's wedding, the video arrived.

I watched the bliss of that afternoon, spellbound by each moment as it came and went: the best man's toast; the maid of honor's memories of her lifelong friend; the nuptial dance; the wedding cake. And the fun, the frolicking, and hellos to me from guests.

Whoever you are that invented the video, I send thanks from the bottom of my heart.

—"Joyride" III, October 23, 1996

My brother tends to be passive and quiet. Me, I'm loud and aggressive. I love the ocean. He doesn't. I run barefoot on the beach. He usually wears black socks and shined shoes. He loves city life. I hate the city.

No. 1 loves chicken; No. 2 finds it depressing.
—"Joyride" II, November 4, 1981

No. 2 rarely goes into the bathroom; No. 1 rarely comes out. To No. 2 the bathroom is to be used only when duty calls and rarely at other times, whereas No. 1 feels he requires innumerable showers and visits to check the mirror there.

—"Joyride" II, January 13, 1982

No. 1 started walking around a year of age, but No. 2 started at seven months.

No. 2 was a jumper. He wore out one baby carriage after another, then one stroller after another because he jumped up and down in them as if they were tumbling mats.

The beautiful hand-carved wooden blocks made in Kentucky that No. 1 had played with were no good for No. 2. No. 1 had liked to build bridges and towers with the blocks, but No. 2 liked to throw them. The wooden blocks were put up in the attic, and No. 2 got a set of brightly colored plastic blocks.

No. 1 had liked fairy tales and Mother Goose. No. 2 did not. He liked how-to books.

When No. 2 went off to kindergarten and I handed him the same little lunchbox No. 1 had carried, he left it behind. It embarrassed him.
—"Joyride" III, October 23, 1985

I guess the only important thing we have in common is our mother. It's hard to define our disparity, but after he married it seemed to grow. I resented the briefness of his and his wife's visits to Mom's house. When they would arrive at noon on a Saturday and depart at four on Sunday afternoon, I'd be really pissed. That he and she had full-time professions in Philadelphia didn't matter to me. "You guys are blue collar workers," his wife once said. "You can do stuff like this. You can walk away from a job, come back later, and pick up where you left off. Keith can't do that. It's nice that you could just pack up and come here, but we can't simply up and leave our lives behind to help out here. Maybe you can, but we can't." Besides her nonchalance, Tara and I didn't appreciate her white-collar/blue-collar comparison. The fact that my wife and I would return to our California home at summer's end didn't enter my mind—and, in fact, when my mother died, neither of her sons, nor her husband, were nearby. Her sister and best friend sat by her side during her final moments of life.

# Mom's Columns

Writers write, I suppose, in whatever way they are able to
devise. Had I lived a million years ago, I wonder if I would have
made squiggles on the walls of caves.
   —"Joyride" III, August 13, 1997

During the final months of her illness, my mom dictated her column to her Hubby, who entered the words into his laptop computer. Then I'd sit next to her and read back a printout of what she
had dictated. She'd make alterations and corrections as if she was
sitting at some newspaper city desk. When she still could, she would
sit in her wheelchair and type on a desktop computer that sat on a
wheel-around bedside table. For more than thirty years, she had
banged out her column on typewriters of every kind and descrip-
tion.

Her columns were probably read at one time or another by
almost everyone who lived or visited Cape May, both the town and
county. Some people clipped them, passed them around, even
traded them like bubble-gum-package baseball cards. My relatives
in far-off places kept tabs on No. 1 and me through columns mailed
to them. Family vacations, holiday happenings, Thanksgiving mis-
haps—all were written about. People have told me they actually collected her columns, as keepsakes from their Cape May vacations.
For as long as the newsprint will last, readers can experience pictur-
esque scenes and memorable moments as seen through the eyes of a
wonderful small town writer. She portrayed Cape May's saltwater

marshes, Victorian structures, premium beaches, summer and wintertime scenes—and its peepers.

There are many things I love about springtime. The most magical, for me, is standing on an old marsh near twilight and listening to the peepers....

> Their wee croaks, sung in unison, to me are the sweetest music of the new season.
>
> Peepers are little frogs that sing mainly at night when the air is warm during March and early April. You listen to the ground, not to the trees....
>
> And the peepers do the rest, orchestrating the spring evening, bringing music to our ears and to our souls.
> —"Joyride" III, March 29, 1995

> For years I sought the places where the peepers would come to perform their chorus.... On early springtime evenings, if you're standing near an old marsh or farmland, you can hear their sweet, delicate songs rising from the earth.
> —"Joyride" III, March 26, 1997

Sometimes it was nice being a sort of hometown celebrity. Sometimes it was awful. For instance, in my junior year in high school, as I was donating blood, I fainted. It was in her column the next week. "No. 2 wants to be a Lifeguard but can't stand the sight of blood," it chortled. Many a time I complained to her about broadcasting details from my private life.

> No. 1 and No. 2 are bottomless inspiration for a writing mother. I have followed them around for years, jotting down their adventures and abusing them in print.
>
> "Mom, this isn't fair," they'd moan. "How could you, Mom? Now everyone knows."
> —"Joyride" III, March 11, 1987

It's no secret No. 2 doesn't always spit out his words the way he intends. For instance, he has a terrible time saying the word "adult." Unfortunately, it seems to come out "dolt."
—"Joyride" II, May 27, 1981

When No. 2 was little, his rubber duckie was uncommonly fascinating to him. He liked to throw rubber duckie into a sink or bathtub. He also liked to fill up basins of water so that he and rubber duckie could play together.
—"Joyride" III, November 20, 1985

During last week's Grammy awards, I sat glued to the TV.... When a special award was announced for Leonard Bernstein, No. 2 wanted to know, "What's a Leonard Bernstein?"
—"Joyride" III, March 13, 1985

I told him I would be giving him my old mattress and getting rid of his mattress. He started to cry. "I love that mattress," he sobbed. "I can float on it; I can pretend I'm on a magic carpet or on a boat."

"It's not like we're giving away a puppy," I said. "It's just a mattress. It's too soft anyhow. My hard mattress will be a lot better for your back."

"What's the matter with my back?" asked No. 2, suddenly alarmed. "Is there something wrong with it? Are you trying to tell me there's something the matter with me? Oh, Mom, what is it?"
—"Joyride" II, January 16, 1980

A long time ago, when No. 2 son was still wet behind the ears, he got all excited when we told a waiter we'd need a doggie bag to take home.

"Are we getting a dog, Mommy?" No. 2 asked while the waiter stood making out the check.
—"Joyride" III, February 2, 1991

# Knife-Wielding Nurse

On August 20, Tara and I went to an elegant restaurant to celebrate our anniversary, temporarily relinquishing our duties as night nurses. After a day of beach guarding, I rode my bike to Colliers Liquor Store and picked out a twenty-dollar bottle of California Merlot. Yes, the restaurant was BYOB (bring your own bottle). As we sipped our wine and savored the wasabi-sauced salmon, mashed potatoes, and fancy vegetables, we also relished our temporary escape from the home that had been turned into a single-patient hospital. We walked home holding hands. As we climbed the brick steps, we heard a loud voice. Someone inside was yelling.

Opening the door, we heard someone chastising someone. It was a substitute nurse, admonishing my mother: "You're too much work; you ask for too many things," she exclaimed, repeating herself several times. I rushed into the room and over to my mom, who was crying hysterically.

"She is treating me badly, Craig," my mom said.

By this time, the nurse had gone down the hallway to the kitchen. I followed her and demanded, "Louisa, what's going on?"

The nurse didn't answer me. She kept chanting, "You're too much work; you ask for too much." As if to change the subject, she began cutting carrots with a knife. She seemed terribly upset—almost hysterical.

Speaking in a low and kindly voice, Tara gently placed her hand on Louisa's shoulder and asked, "What can we do to help you?"

As if she hadn't heard, Louisa gripped the knife tightly and huffed, "I'll take care of her complaining. Yes, I will take care of it."

As Louisa motioned hysterically, Tara stepped back and demanded, "What the hell are you talking about?"

Louisa walked toward the doorway and I grabbed her wrist. "Let go of the knife," I said. She wouldn't. Her strength was surprising and scared me. "Let go of the knife," I asserted, twisting her left wrist, but she continued to hold it tightly. "Please, Louisa, put the knife down," I pleaded. My plea, or the passing moments, seemed to cool her anger, or whatever was bothering her. She dropped the knife to the kitchen floor and went to the telephone on the kitchen wall. She dialed 911. "What are you doing?" I demanded. Then she hung up, not saying another word. Within a few moments, the phone rang. It was the operator.

"We just received a call from you," he said.

"Well I didn't call," I answered.

"Someone called."

"Well, I didn't."

"Who did?"

"The nurse, Louisa did," I said, annoyed.

"Why did she call?" he asked.

"I don't know why, why don't you ask her?" I said. I handed her the telephone in disgust.

She then told them I was trying to kill her with a knife. Within five minutes, two Cape May police officers arrived. They briefly questioned Louisa and then me. "Are you trying to kill your mother's nurse?" one officer asked.

"No, obviously," I replied.

"Why did she call?" he asked.

"Because she is crazy," I said.

"But why did she call, even if she is crazy?" he asked.

"What kind of question is that?" I snapped, sarcastically, which probably wasn't a good idea. Everyone knows that when the highway patrol pulls you over to the side of the road, being sarcastic will simply get you a bigger fine or a night in jail. As the other cop glared at me, I recognized him from our high school days. We were on the wrestling team together. In wrestling matches, he was a relentless opponent. Suddenly I got the feeling he'd treat me not as a fellow alumnus but as an opponent needing to be pinned to the floor. In my mind, I envisioned him and his fellow officer tag-teaming me to certain defeat, with me, the loser, hauled before a judge at Cape May Courthouse the next day.

When they questioned Louisa a second time, I realized I had a chance of escaping certain imprisonment. She acted crazy. As she ranted and cussed in some African tongue, both policemen appeared puzzled. I doubt they understood a word she yelled.

Next, they questioned Tara. She spoke calmly: "This is all a misunderstanding," she said. I watched through the screen door as they stared at her breasts and didn't once look in her eyes. After five minutes of staring and listening, they told Tara we should all go back to bed, and to call 911 if there was any more trouble. Tara assured them everything would be just fine. Louisa stormed upstairs and apparently went immediately to sleep. Me, I lay awake next to Mom and fantasized about ways to send Louisa packing, and what it would be like to paddle in the middle of the ocean.

Little did I realize, the altercation had been a deliberate set-up. Louisa needed an excuse to quit the job of caring for my mother. She'd planned the whole incident. Louisa never intended to harm my mother. Carelessly swinging that knife around, though, she could have slashed Tara, herself, or me. We didn't know it at the time, but the agency that supplied our nurses had a rule that they couldn't just fail to show up for work or simply give an employer notice of leaving. This agency took pride in the dependability of its nurses. If a nurse didn't have an approved reason for absence or quitting, the agency barred her from all future work. This meant almost certain deportation by federal immigration authorities, to which the agency would report the errant nurse. Eventually, we learned Louisa wanted to move to Brooklyn, New York, to join her family that had recently arrived from Africa. Also, in the weeks following her departure, a bunch of bill collectors showed up. She owed thousands of dollars. Evidently, she knew they were catching up to her.

# The "Paddle" Obsession

The "paddle" became an obsession. I sought information about the bay and the nearby ocean from anyone I could find who had sailed on them—fishermen, sailors, boaters, swimmers, whoever. One was an old high school buddy who worked aboard the Cape May Ferry that sails across Delaware Bay regularly. A graduate of the Merchant Marine Academy, he had been around boats his entire life. I figured he must know the bay trek like the back of his hand. When he heard I planned to paddle it, his big eyes bulged. "You crazy," he exclaimed. "Those currents will eat you up."

I was not dissuaded. "C'mon, Stevie, I'm sure I can do it. I just need to time the tide. It won't be all that hard, will it?" I asked.

"Let's just say," he advised, "the ocean needs to be calm—and you still need to avoid those shoals. You're going to need boats. You need some safety boats with you." Boats? Sure, boats. Why didn't I think of that?

"Oh yeah, we have some boats; you better believe it," I said, as if there actually were boats signed up for a genuine project.

I figured the more I acted like I knew what I was talking about, the more people would think I knew what I was doing. The buzz started around the beach with the guards in Headquarters. Guards came up to me periodically and asked what I was doing and if they could be involved. I said "yes" to everyone: kayakers, paddle boarders, and even two mothers, one a lifeguard and one a lifeguard's wife, who wanted to row across the bay.

Kim, a young mother, was a lifeguard and an excellent athlete. She was short with striking black and sun-bleached curly hair that came down to the small of her back. Every muscle in her body was defined. Kim had a daughter and a son and was in the process of getting a divorce from her estranged husband, a cook at the Crab House in Atlantic City. She worked out constantly.

Kim had rowed around the island before with Katherine, who grew up in Montreal and had rowing in her blood. Her husband, Herb, was a tall German who had the body of a twenty-year-old, yet was pushing sixty. He taught Katherine how to row and how to row correctly. With a stiff German accent, a cold stare, and curt coaching calls, he'd trained her well. Herb was primarily a skull rower but carried his skills over to lifeguard rowing on the open ocean. She rowed mostly in the ocean and had great endurance. She was small and petite, but taller than Kim. She had three sons and a French accent. Her hair was short, almost like a boy's, and she had stunning cheekbones and beautiful dark eyes. They rowed together all summer. Whether the waves were flat or huge, I would see them training in the morning and after work in the evening.

Kim had a blank stare when she rowed stern. Katherine seemed full of emotion, yelling out directions. It was natural to have these women participating in The Paddle. They were strong and full of energy. I was attracted to strong women: women who had muscles, women who had an opinion, women who could beat me in swims or runs or raise two kids by themselves without the help of an alcoholic father.

# *Wonder Woman and the Ayatollah*

Early on, my mom did what she could to make ends meet. To earn a little money, she babysat, cared for invalid neighbors, and worked part-time at a law office downtown. Some years, after my father left us, she got food stamps and welfare payments. She never liked "being on welfare," as she called it, deeming it "charity that others more needy should be getting." Whenever she could get work that didn't interfere with what she considered her ability to raise her kids properly, she worked. When we were older, she did clerical work and copy editing for the *Cape May Star & Wave* newspaper. Later, she worked for the *Wildwood Gazette-Leader* and finally the *Cape May County Herald* group of newspapers.

After she got us kids off to school, she rode her three-wheel bike to the law office, where she typed letters, did clerical work. Later, while working at the local newspapers, she did copy editing and secretarial stuff. Her column was always written on her own time, usually at home. In effect, she was a freelance writer.

My mother nicknamed my absent father, "Ayatollah Khomeini" or simply "The Ayatollah." The real Ayatollah Khomeini was a religious leader and political dictator who dominated Iran in the 1950s, when Americans were held captive at the United States embassy there. In the United States, his name came to be synonymous with contempt.

My father's name is Mark Forrest. He's a media jack-of-all-trades. Originally, my father's name was Milton O. Fenkel (the "O" stood for Overs, which is a story in itself). He changed his name. It's not unusual for people to change their names, of course. It's common in show business. Writers and authors often use a "pen name." Early on, my father realized that, unless you were David Sarnoff or Leonard Goldenson, having a Jewish name wasn't a big asset in the broadcast business. So he changed it to Mark Forrest.

After he changed it, he worked for radio stations, where he did everything from news writing to making coffee. In time, he grew into a more-or-less famous Philadelphia TV personality. His downfall came after he became editor of a wine and spirits publication. His job involved showing up at everyone's wine tasting parties. As soon as he walked into a bar or club, his drinks were on the house. Every day was open house at the nation's breweries, wineries, and distilleries. Consequently, he became a connoisseur of fine wines, expensive whiskeys, and other spirited beverages—and a horrible alcoholic. He got some great jobs after that, but they all ended in self-inflicted disaster. Eventually, he was broke, out of work, divorced, deeply in debt, alienated from his children, in poor health, in jail, and virtually blacklisted in the radio-TV community. He had his fifteen minutes of fame and he drank it away.

In later years, he did show up in Cape May occasionally to whisk my brother and me to his house in South Philadelphia, two hours away. Now and then, we'd spend a weekend there. He was always late for our pick-up. Too many Sunday afternoons were spent waiting, waiting, waiting. He'd promise to arrive at noon Saturday, and show up at four or five in the afternoon. Except when he didn't show up at all. Getting to his house around seven-thirty, we would eat pizza and rummage through his library of movies or click up and down the pirated cable channels, watch something or other, and fall asleep around midnight.

Sunday morning he slept until eleven-thirty. My brother and I were wide awake by eight o'clock. Once awake, he would smoke multiple cigarettes and read the *Sunday Inquirer* until he found enough strength to decide what we could do that day. By that time there wasn't much we could do, as it was near time to be driven back to Cape May. By the time we got home, our clothes stunk of cigarette smoke. It became a ritual: taking our clothes off the minute we got into the house and putting them into the washing machine. Mom questioned us the minute we got in the door:

"Did he feed you kids?" she'd ask.

"Yes," No. 1 would answer.

"What did you eat?" she'd ask.

"Pizza," I'd say.

"That's all, nothing else?" she'd half ask and half exclaim.

"Beer, cigarettes, a big jar of pickles," I'd joke.

Then, Mom would laugh and say something like, "As long as you had a good time."

From previous inquisitions, she knew we probably didn't get to bed until midnight and that he didn't wake up until eleven-thirty the next morning, while we stared at his pirated cable channels and had Entenmann's cheese pastry and diet soda for breakfast.

> Before No. 1 and No. 2 get into the covered wagon for their weekends away, they fill a jug with local water, claiming urban water makes them sick.
> —"Joyride" II, December 18, 1981

# The Spanish Bull

My grandfather, Mark Forrest's father, Milton O. Fenkel Sr., was a self-made man who spent little time with his son. He was a world traveler. His wife and child weren't. He and my grandmother, Dorothy, shooshed the junior Milton off to private boarding schools. Should I blame my father for not knowing how to have a loving and considerate relationship with his sons when his father had taught him nothing about that? Should I appreciate that my father always seemed to be trying to imitate some mythological image he had of his own father? Amazing though he was, my grandfather, Mickey, never could have been the Apollo my father imagined him to be. Nobody could. A golden gloves boxer and black belt karate fighter in his youth, Mickey leaped from dentist to African safari medical advisor to physician and teacher at New York University and other medical schools. He invented and patented some weird toothbrush that simultaneously cleaned both sides of your molars. Tired of being a dentist when he was sixty-four years old, he enrolled in medical school and graduated when he was seventy. After practicing medicine in Madrid, Spain, Mickey returned to America and taught neuromuscular surgery until he was eighty.

"You used to fight with grandfather all the time," said No. 2.

"Yes," I said. "He argued with everybody. But it's funny, now that he's gone, I get a yen now and then for a really good argument."

"Well," said No. 2. "If you want to have a fight with somebody, I could make a gift card for you entitling you to one good fight with me."

—"Joyride" II, December 22, 1982

Members of my family used to say I was the only one who could get along with him. He was a fighter all right. You could hardly say "good morning" to him without getting into a real good knockdown, drag-out contest.

Every couple of years he would come back from Spain for a visit…. We'd be arguing at the airport before his suitcase arrived on the conveyor belt….

He wasn't your everyday kind of father-in-law. You didn't point him to the nearest rocking chair and make light conversation.

—"Joyride" III, December 16, 1992

After my mother and father divorced, Mickey continued to keep in touch with my mom, my brother, and me. I'd read the letters he scribbled and sent via international mail. She too thought he was amazing. However, when he did come to visit us, the two of them argued nonstop. My mom loved a good argument. So did he. Like two Spanish bulls, they clashed horns on a regular basis. I remember him waiting outside the bathroom door one afternoon, to finish an argument they'd started in the early hours of the morning.

# Boats and Waves

Tara was really getting into rowing lifeguard boats. She felt invigorated by moving such a massive boat in the ocean. The lifeguard boats in South Jersey are called Vanduynes, named after Dick Vanduyne. The boat weighs about six hundred pounds and stretches about fourteen feet long. It's made of fiberglass and allows one or two rowers. Wood is layered around the gunnels. Oarlocks are two pieces of metal stretched in the shape of a "u" so that the oars fit snugly in them. The boat has a long legacy. Riding waves in them can be dangerous. During stormy conditions, people in them have closely escaped death—including me. The amount of force the boat has behind it when pushed by a wave is tremendous.

One chilly morning in July, a senior citizen and his wife walked up to my lifeguard stand. "Are you Craig?" he asked. "My name's Bill. I was wondering if I could do that paddle with you." With his long white beard and thick white hair, he reminded me of Charlton Heston playing Moses in *The Ten Commandments* movie.

"Like help out you mean…?" I asked.

"Well, sure, but I want to paddle it—and I have a boat," he said. After explaining that he was a professor at a nearby college who often kayaked in the bay and ocean, he told me he had always yearned to paddle from Delaware to Cape May.

"I've even dreamt about it," he said.

"Huh? Dreamt about it? What do you mean?" I inquired.

"Well," he went on, "dreams or nightmares; in them, I'm never able to finish the paddle. Something always happens." Amazingly, I had had similar dreams. That we both dreamt about paddling made me feel instantly comfortable with this guy.

A professor in the winter, Bill was a guide for Aqua Trails in the summer. Besides himself, he had several friends who also wanted to do The Paddle. I told him "the more the merrier" but that they all had to be in excellent physical shape. I also told him they needed to solicit money from sponsors. By this time I had decided The Paddle would be a fundraising event, to help offset my mother's tremendous medical bills not covered by insurance.

Paddle ideas flooded my mind all the time. First, I focused on paddlers, then on community awareness, and, finally, on getting contributions. We got volunteers aplenty. Local newspapers publicized the coming event. As for fundraising, people were either ambivalent or excited about The Paddle; the latter group was ready to help in any way.

A sense of unity was starting to formulate. The day after Bill and I talked, I told my family some kayakers planned to paddle also. When my stepbrother, who Mom identified as Stepson No. 1 in her column, heard this, he became interested. He wanted to paddle across the bay in his two-person fold-up kayak. At summer's beginning, he and The Hubby, his dad, had kayaked along the Cape May canal. A lawyer from Philadelphia, Stepson No. 1 and his wife came on weekends to visit my mom and help out. At Howard University, the almost all-black college where Stepson No. 1 studied law, he was the only white guy in his graduating class. During The Paddle Tara and Stepson No. 1 manned his two-man kayak. He wasn't in great shape, but I knew Tara could probably pull him along if necessary.

# Rough Water Ahead

My family decided, since I had put The Paddle wheels in motion, they might as well all get involved. At a family conference in our backyard, No. 1 son, who had scoffed at my idea, designated himself the event's "publicity man." This was somewhat logical. He was then Beaver College's director of public relations. The Hubby volunteered his support as well, although he previously had rejected my idea as "too risky." My mother agreed it was very risky, but seeing as how the event was a *fait accompli*, she gave it her blessing. At the backyard conference, Tara and No. 1 stepson talked about his kayak. The Hubby discussed setting up a charitable foundation for tax purposes.

No. 1 son wrote a press release headlined, "Lifeguards To Surf Across Bay" and handed me a printout. After I read it, I corrected him: "We aren't surfing across the bay. We're paddling."

He told me that for publicity purposes it was better to say surfing. "Most editors and news directors won't know what paddling is," he said.

"But Keith, we are paddling, not surfing!" was my angry response.

"What do you know about press releases?" he snapped.

I took the piece of paper, crumpled it up, and threw it at his face. I was boiling mad. Squinting, he glared momentarily, then lunged. I met him halfway, grabbing the collar of his red shirt. In brotherly anguish, my left fist headed toward his face. The Hubby hollered and jumped between us. I held on tightly to No. 1's shirt. Shaking with anger, I was determined to take down big brother. Tara shouted, "Knock it off Craig." Her voice caused me to freeze, pull back, and let go of Keith's shirt. No. 1 said, "Go back to California with your idealistic wife." The Hubby sat on the grass, tears rolling down his face. The stress from mom dying was building up inside everyone. I was making it worse, I thought. My mom told me, "Calm down and hold it together."

Walking toward the beach by myself, my heart was pounding and my breath went in and out in huffs and puffs. As I neared the ocean, the rhythmic sound of crashing waves eased my temper a bit. When I saw the water, I felt better and began to breathe normally. My knees sank as I said to myself, "I will not compromise; I will not compromise; I will not compromise…."

The next day, t-shirts were being printed that read, "Paddle Across The Bay: An Awareness For Lou Gehrig's disease." On the front of the shirt was a black silhouette of my mom riding a three-wheel bike, the same drawing that was atop her "Joyride" column every week. As word about the coming Paddle spread, letters to my mom poured in from her fans, friends, and relatives. Many spoke of how much her writing meant to them. Some included a contribution. Mail delivery became enjoyable. Instead of dreading the opening of envelopes, because so many recent ones had contained bad news, I looked forward to opening them.

> Weeks ago they told me their plan to hold a "paddle across the Delaware" event to raise funds toward my medical expenses. I was doubtful, but they were determined. They pulled it together, involving the community in a way I never dreamed could happen.
> This, their gift to me, to show their tenaciousness and love.
> —"Joyride" III, August 27, 1997

As August 23, the date of The Paddle, neared, weather patterns were changing on the Eastern Seaboard. Tropical storms began to form off the Lesser Antilles, and headed northeast toward Cape May. The city of Cape May is an island at the very bottom of New Jersey. One side of it faces the Atlantic Ocean. As autumn approached, things began churning in the Atlantic. For Cape May lifeguards, rescues became more frequent. Rip currents that previously came maybe once a day became constant. Swells were pushing in almost every day. A warming ocean provided fuel for hurricanes, which feed off the warmest currents. Cape May's water temperature was then at a record-breaking seventy-nine degrees Fahrenheit.

As the summer beach season drew to a close, I focused on paddle logistics, such as arranging for two safety boats to accompany the paddlers. One was named *Emotional Rescue*. Its owner was Kurt Henry, a longtime lifeguard well into his fifties. He made money doing TV commercials. I think he was the voice for Tony the Tiger. A huge man who wore the skimpiest shorts on the beach, he had a hairpiece that sometimes fell off when he went swimming. In the middle of the day, Kurt rowed a lifeguard boat back and forth in front of the busiest swimming beaches. Occasionally, sweating profusely and panting loudly, he'd pull up to the beach I was guarding. I'd try not to stare at him, because if I did he'd likely ask for me to help pull his heavy boat up to dry sand. The times I did help, he paraded his short shorts and noticeable belly before the middle-aged beach bunnies.

Bill McCarther owned the second boat, the *Anaerobic*. During The Paddle, it was captained by an old local named Deacon. In his sixties and bald, Deacon was shaped like a tugboat. During the non-summer months he drove a school bus in Philadelphia. He was someone I confided in nearly every day.

After signing up the safety boats, I concentrated on charting the course. Terry Randolph offered to help me. I sat at his house one night under a hurricane lantern because there was a power outage. We had strewn ocean maps over his dining room table. We drank whisky and discussed the outgoing and incoming tides. He volunteered to captain the *Emotional Rescue* because Kurt had expressed concern about driving his million-dollar boat amid the difficult conditions that were looming.

When my clock went off at six the next morning, the weatherman said there was a tropical storm named "Faith" making its way up the coast. My stomach sank as I heard the news, and my eyes fluttered nonstop. I shot out of bed unbalanced and ran down to the kitchen. Tara was already making coffee and getting a bag packed for her day of guarding. I asked her if she'd heard about the storm. She answered, "Yes," and suggested I postpone The Paddle. I told her it was too early to tell.

That day the waves were big and the rip currents were relentless. Swimmers were getting sucked out constantly. One minute the ocean would look glassy and peaceful; the next minute a hard-running brown river would split the ocean and suck out anything and anyone in its way. Around noon, two beaches down, I saw two guards standing up, holding their lifesaving torpedoes, ready to enter the water. From their lifeguard stand I saw a hundred-yard rip current flowing faster than any I'd ever seen. In the middle, it was ripping like a balloon on a windy day.

There was a woman struggling. I immediately knew this was going to be a serious rescue. I grabbed the paddleboard and the torpedo and sprinted down the beach. My legs burned as I dragged the heavy board behind me. When I finally arrived, the woman was two hundred yards from the beach and going under. Three guards were in the water struggling to get to her. I shot onto my board and took the rip right out to her. As she was going under, I grabbed her by her hair. I jumped off my board and tried to get my arms around her waist. I couldn't. She was too big, weighing maybe three hundred pounds. At that point, fifteen lifeguards and a lifeguard boat were in the water. Terry and Herb were rowing the boat and Terry screamed, "Put her in the boat, Craig!"

"She is not going in the boat, Terry," I said.

"Put her in the boat now," he said sternly.

"No, Terry she's too big; I can't get her out of the water." Herb agreed: "Terry, she's not going in the boat."

She was screaming and coughing, and had started to turn blue. As the guards formed a human chain, I grabbed her by her neck as if corralling a bull. She screamed, "You're choking me; let go." Each guard moaned and hissed as they pulled her to shore. The current was fierce and each pull tugged on my shoulder, which was attached to a line. We finally made it in and she collapsed on the wet sand. The beach ambulance crew strapped her down on a board and rushed her to the hospital. Every guard was visibly disturbed and shaken. As the boat came in, an eight-foot wave hit it broadside, sending Terry and Herb flipping through the shore break. Luckily, no one was hurt.

# The Paddle

That night everyone's emotions were high. The captain of the Beach
Patrol was not happy that many guards would be taking off on a day
when they would be needed. Later that night, I could hardly sleep. I
heard the waves pounding and the wind howling. I walked up to the
beach and asked God to protect us on our journey. The waves had
covered every ounce of sand. As I walked back, tears fell from my
eyes. I wondered if I was endangering my life and the lives of my
friends.

At five a.m., I packed my gear, including a long-sleeved Lycra
rash guard to protect my arms and back from the sun, a visor, and
lots of sun-protection glop and drinking water. No. 1 stepson and
Tara woke up at six in good spirits. Tara thought we should postpone, but I wanted to see the ocean before making a decision to put
it off for another time. By six-thirty the phone was ringing nonstop.
I walked to the living room and silently held mom's hand. We spent
about twenty minutes not saying anything. We just looked into one
another's eyes. She told me to be careful, without moving her
mouth. I kissed her on the forehead and told her I would be back
soon. Tara and No. 1 stepson told her that it was her day and she
was coming with us in spirit.

We were in the Beach Patrol Headquarters by seven-thirty a.m.
for a briefing: five paddle boarders, seven kayakers, and two rowers.
The paddle boarders went downstairs and got their boards ready.
Other non-participants were filtering into the building. It was low
tide and the surf didn't appear too angry. The sun was already blaz-

ing, and the sky was clear. Everyone including myself felt we should go forward with The Paddle. The gear was being piled into two beach patrol trucks. Someone screamed from the back of the beach that a boy was having trouble getting to shore. Dan and I jumped from the back of the truck and ran toward the ocean. The boy was going under quick. Dan got into the water before me and held onto the boy, comforted him. I helped pull both of them in. Tensions rose as we escorted the boy from the ocean. The captain looked down ominously at us from the top deck and shook his head.

We huddled in both trucks and drove to the pier where *Emotional Rescue* and *Anaerobic* were waiting. The lifeguard boat had to be picked up from the ocean. We were going to tow it behind *Emotional Rescue*. The rowboat was packed; three paddleboards, water, and rope. I sat on *Emotional Rescue* with Tara, Terry, No. 1 stepson, Dan, Shawn, and Kurt. We headed southeast toward the Headquarters to pick up the boat. The waves were breaking off the jetty as we headed toward the beach. Two guards swam the boat out to us. We tied it to our boat so we could tow it to Delaware. The waves were smacking *Emotional Rescue*. Terry was yelling orders out to us. The tricky part was lining up the rowboat behind the *Anaerobic*'s motor so it wouldn't eat up our towline. The swells became larger. We headed out to sea. The boat rocked, and my stomach turned nauseously. I looked over at Tara and she gave me a seasick smile. I was quiet, thinking about our journey. Halfway to Delaware, the *Anaerobic* was spotted in the distance. We met them and yelled, "Hello!"

Twenty minutes later, the boats dropped us off about a quarter-mile from the beach so we could arrange our equipment. Kim and Katherine jumped into the boat and started rowing it toward the beach. On the beach, Tara and No. 1 stepson assembled their portable suitcase kayak. I stretched in the hot sand. Shawn and Dan sat on the beach preparing their water supply. Bill and the kayakers adjusted their paddles and seat harnesses. We were all itching to get going. The two boats idled and waited patiently for us. Finally, after a half-hour, which seemed like an eternity, our flotilla assembled.

Our spirits were high, and the ocean was beautiful. The sky was clear, and it was so peaceful. Soon we were seeing brown pelicans graze the ocean, and super tankers in the distance. Kim and Katherine rowed and pounded every stroke with a clean swipe of their blades. The boats were throwing us bottles of water when we needed them. The kayakers had it easy in my eyes. Katherine and Kim were leading, with the kayakers not too far behind them—and then the slow paddle boarders. We were using our hands as paddles; so we were much slower.

Two hours into the trip the seas took a noticeable turn, and the swells were increasing. Soon, instead of paddling straight, we were paddling up and down, riding the swells. We were losing one another. The clouds started to form over our heads. The heat had been intense early in the trip, but now a slight breeze could be felt from the south. Our main concern was avoiding the shoals. The shoals were about seven miles off of Cape May. Aptly titled "Dead Man's Shoals," they had been the cause of many boat wrecks in the Atlantic. There was no sense to the waves that broke in Dead Man's. They broke sideways and the currents were relentless. Even the best swimmers couldn't survive if Dead Man's was bad. Originally, our intent was to paddle against the tide halfway through our trip and then have the approaching high tide swing us around.

The storm was approaching. It was getting more difficult as we headed straight for the shoals. Kurt Henry was throwing up his guts in the bathroom of the boat. Terry announced on a megaphone that maybe we should consider calling this off. I said, "No," and immediately looked for Tara's approval. She was sitting in the bow of the two-man kayak looking tired. No. 1 stepson was delirious. The waves were knocking back and forth. The single kayakers were fairing pretty well. Katherine and Kim were still pumping their strokes.

My arms felt like rubber. We had only gone nine miles. I kept thinking of failure and seeing my mother in her bed, pinned down by her disease. I needed to do this. I needed to feel the accomplishment. There was no turning back. Dead Man's was approaching us and it covered a half-mile radius. The boats could not follow us in because it was too shallow.

The sky darkened even more. Kim and Katherine were the first to enter the shoals. Katherine's head tweaked like an ostrich looking for a safe route while waves banged the back of the boat, nailing them sideways. Minutes before, Shawn had felt ill and climbed onto *Emotional Rescue*. Now Terry was paddling in Shawn's place. Terry yelled to Kim and Katherine to row straight through the waves, but it was just too difficult for them. Next, the kayakers entered that pit of hell, and the currents swung them around so hard they were going into it stern-first. I yelled to Tara to follow Kim and Katherine. I picked up my stroke and tried to shadow them. I was weak, and Terry was fresher. He sprinted ahead of me, and stayed close behind them. The boats floated helplessly around the perimeter of the shoals, and my throat felt tight and swollen.

A wave traveling from the east met a solid wave traveling from the west, and the resulting force banged Kim and Katherine's boat hard. It was thrown up out of the water and slammed down on its side. Katherine hit her head and Kim lost her oars. Tara and No. 1 stepson sprinted for the boat. Terry followed closely. Another wave hit the boat. Now they were missing all their oars. Tara picked up two while I screamed, "Fuck the oars, Tara! Let's get out of here!" Hit by a wave, the kayak's keel slammed right into Terry's board, which now had a hole in it. Tara and No. 1 stepson kept fishing out Katherine's and Kim's oars and throwing them back to them.

The kayakers and Dan had taken an alternate route and already were safe outside of Dead Man's. The waves got bigger and more unpredictable. At one point, I was riding some of the waves on my belly to stay close to everyone, when I went right under and lost my board. I freaked. All I could think about were those dreams at my mother's house: the water, the rush, and the darkness. My lungs were tight and my spirits were down. Then I snapped, and my adrenaline took over. I sprinted for my board ten yards away. I inched up close and grabbed it. The six of us were helpless in Dead Man's hands.

The shoals let up for a few minutes, and we powered toward open water. Katherine was bleeding on the side of her face and Terry's board was taking in water. I was shivering and coughing. Tara and No.1 stepson were visibly distraught and winded. Two waves knocked us out of the shoals, and now the boats were turning around toward us. Kurt Henry was wiping throw-up from his mouth and asking, "Do any of you want to come on board?" Everyone refused. We had five miles to go and we heard thunder in the distance. You could see the lighthouse on the horizon. I was so glad Terry was with me. We paddled stroke for stroke. Kim, Katherine, Johnny, and Tara were warriors. Blood collected in Katherine's eyes, but she kept rowing.

Soon the lighthouse got bigger and bigger, and we saw our other party. The swells were now fifteen feet and the current was moving at twenty-five knots. We tried to head straight for the Headquarters but swung toward the cement ship. The current was harder than ever. We hugged the beach. I began to feel as if I was hallucinating. We headed around the last jetty. Hundreds of people lined the beach. The loudspeaker system announced our arrival. The waves were thick and pounding off the jetty. We were three hours late and the sun was starting to set. Sirens were blazing on the beach and people cheered as kayakers made their way in, riding huge waves. Most wiped out and rolled in toward the beach. Two guards swam out to Katherine and Kim and helped them steer through the gigantic waves. Tara and No. 1 stepson took off on a barreling wave and flipped dangerously close to a disposal pipe. Terry and I were next, riding a wave in together.

# Heartfelt Victory

My feet touched the Cape May sand, as people cheered and rushed toward us. Press photographers took pictures of us. Lightning cracked in the distance. *Anaerobic* and *Emotional Rescue* sat offshore, ready to take port. No. 1 stepson insisted on getting his video camera and cell phone from *Emotional Rescue*. Terry and Dan rowed a boat back out to *Emotional Rescue* and grabbed No. 1 stepson's gear. Mom's Hubby hugged Tara, and everyone involved joined hands and created a circle. Nothing was said. We just held hands quietly as lightning struck the ocean and lit up the background. I ran to Mom's house in my bare feet, every breath hurting. After I'd ran ten blocks, my toes were bloodied. I threw open the door and cried on her limp shoulder.

> This afternoon, August 17, an armada completed a seventeen-mile paddle across the Delaware Bay. Five hours after casting off at Lewes, Delaware, this flotilla arrived at beach patrol headquarters in Cape May.
>
> No. 2 son, his wife, my stepson, and a brigade of determined paddlers set out on this hot, muggy Sunday to complete their mission on my behalf. No doubt, they'll all sleep well tonight.
>
> —"Joyride" III, August 20, 1997

My water children, No. 2 son and his wife, are about to head back to California. They have been with us since early summer…While helping me cope with my illness, they spent their days working as lifeguards on the Cape May Beach Patrol. They spent many nights sleeping here by me, comforting me, smoothing pillows and giving sips of water.

    —"Joyride" III, August 27, 1997

# *Goodbye*

Three weeks after The Paddle, Tara and I headed home to California in tears. We were both enrolled in college, and classes were about to start. I knew mom was near death. Her body looked hollow. If anyone was in there, it wasn't her; she'd left months earlier. She was doped up on morphine and suffering from occasional dementia.

I was told that she just peacefully closed her eyes and stopped breathing. There was nothing else to do. It was so hard for her, for them, for me, for me—for me. Her sister, Aunt Yonia, and her friend, Mary Riley, were with her at the very end. We weren't home in Santa Cruz longer than a week when No. 1 stepson's wife called and told us that Mom had passed away in her sleep.

I was back on a plane the following day with Tara. Mom had asked to be cremated. She wanted her ashes spread in the ocean off the beach down the street from our house. Her late friend Alma's ashes were spread off that beach and she thought that was a good idea. It went with her philosophy of living and appreciating the earth, the moon, the tide, the love, and the weather that had brought her to that little island she called home. She was reading Rachael Carson's *Silent Spring* before anyone even knew what Earth Day was, and by moving to the shore she was declaring her love for the ocean, the saltwater marsh, and small town living.

Her body was taken to the Evoy's Funeral Home and cremated there. Bill Evoy, an old friend of No. 1's, hand-delivered the urn to our house on Friday. Tara and I gathered around the urn in the dining room and stared at it endlessly. Friends and relatives were storming the house. Her home was never quite private because I was featured in her column so often; I guess I'd always accepted that lack of privacy. At this moment, however, I yearned for absolute solitude. But I didn't get it. Aunt Bella, Cousin Sharon, and Uncle Eli arrived full of bags and tears. Friends, neighbors, fans of the column, lifeguard buddies, and my son's grandmother—they arrived in hoards for a memorial service on the Cape May beachfront. For the ceremony, No. 1 son picked out one of Mom's columns to read. Me, I wrote something I felt my mom would enjoy. Sitting in her big leather chair, overlooking the backyard where she had so often shouted at me, "The game's over, Craig. Come home," during hectic childhood jailbreak games, I grasped one of her ballpoint pens and wrote a short eulogy:

> *Summers on the beach,*
> *my kids at my side,*
> *my diary in my bag,*
> *my hubby on the way.*
> *Now that's a day.*

Not very poetic I suppose, but in her own writing she always strove for simplicity. All she'd want in a eulogy, I figured, was for everyone to relish, as she had, life's really important things, and to savor the fond memories they had shared.

Each of the bereaved seemed to go his own way to the beach. Some drove; some walked; I rode my bike. About fifty showed up, not counting the onlookers who stared from the boardwalk. We held hands, creating an oblong circle, with the urn at the center. No. 1 spoke first, then mom's Hubby, then me. Waves crashed on the beach and sea spray gently grazed over everyone's clothes. We placed the ashes in a bag. I swirled my hand into it, clenching a handful of ashes. My mother's body had been reduced to a little bag of dust. In my hand, the ashes felt lighter than a feather, yet heavier than my heart. They were almost invisible to the naked eye. No. 1 stood there like a statue. His scalp was sunburned and his eyes were wet with tears. Clouds shadowed the sky as the waves continued pounding the beach. I kneeled on the sand and stared at No. 1. It all has come down to this, I thought. No. 1 was the favorite, the smart one, collegiate, responsible, and a realist. No. 2 was reckless, ambivalent, hedonistic, irresponsible, and most of all a dreamer. Two brothers so different it's hard to imagine they had shared the same womb. There were distances between us that we never talked about, and probably never wanted to talk about. Why it came to mind then, I don't know. Why was I having such a troubled, bizarre thought when I should have been mourning Mom?

Hubby walked out onto the slippery jetty, holding a handful of her ashes. Slimy green moss covered the tops of the rocks. He stepped gingerly upon the steep edges, one at a time. He wanted to get as far from the beach as he could, so that all the ashes would be scattered into the ocean, not onto sand, rocks, or someone's clothes.

Hubby neared the end of the jetty and I screamed inside, because I knew how risky it was to be out there. For him, this was uncharted territory. I had been there. I knew how hazardous it was. Though I realized he wanted to be by himself, saying his final goodbyes, maybe I should have accompanied him. Maybe I should have stopped him. I know he didn't want me out there holding his hand so he wouldn't slip, but here was a grief-stricken guy walking someplace he wasn't meant to walk. Here was a guy overcome with loss of his wife and best friend. They dearly loved one another.

After they married, they never argued face-to-face, only over long-distance telephone calls. This was so different from when the Ayatollah lived with us. They argued almost constantly, resulting in a bitter separation and divorce. Since as far back as I remember, The

Hubby was a friend of the family. He had been my father's business partner. His ex-wife had been a longtime friend of my mother's, and he was the best man at my parents' wedding. He met my mother years before his first marriage, and always said he fell in love with her at first sight. "Back then," he'd say, "a nice Irish Catholic boy never dated a nice Jewish girl, let alone married her." Times change.

One day they drove to the end of the beachfront. It was raining. Hubby was wearing his yellow slicker. They watched the stormy waves hit the jetty and spray back onto the rocks. He got out of the car for a better look at the waves. As he walked out onto the slippery rocks and seemed to lose his footing, my mom cringed. She didn't see this as foolhardy so much as adventurous. She later told me this was the day she had a revelation—"an epiphany," she called it—that she and he would marry and live happily ever after. Eighteen years later, he was back on the same rocks, saying goodbye. Suddenly, he slipped, slamming his foot and leg against the jagged rocks. A hoarse "John!" floated out of my mouth. The Hubby was a big man, good shape, walked a lot. He pulled himself up quickly, the leg of his pants covered with green slime. His palms were skinned, slightly bloody, but no bones broken. Except for a swollen ankle that persisted for a few weeks, he was fine. I guess my mom was looking out for him; she was there for him just like he had been there for her. She might have been dismayed that he even climbed out on the rocks in the first place, but probably figured he was just being adventurous again.

Tara held my hand softly as I looked past the rocks for a sign, anything—and there it was. The gray clouds dispersed slowly, about a quarter of a mile past the jetty. A beam of sunlight illuminated the water. I knew she was acknowledging our little ceremony.

# Fuzzy Bunny Slippers

My son didn't attend my mom's funeral, but his other grandmother was there. At that time, she and her fiancé operated a restaurant named the Rio Station. Located in Rio Grande, a town some four miles inland, the restaurant building was formerly a Pennsylvania Reading Seashore Lines train depot. They invited our entire extended family and friends to have dinner there after the ceremony. Cousin Sharon, a railroad buff, was delighted. The restaurant was loaded with train memorabilia. Pictures of steam locomotives and antique railroad signs decorated the walls. The wait staff wore uniforms reminiscent of locomotive engineers' and train conductors.'

In the middle of the restaurant they set up a long table just for us. After two hours of good food and noteworthy hospitality, it was time for our thoughtful and generous hosts to begin catering to their regular clientele. We knew it was time to go when a band began setting up. As drums and electric guitars were carried in, a tall thin woman placed a sign in front of us that read: "Now featuring The Fuzzy Bunny Slippers." Another sign placed nearby said: "Dollar Budweisers" and "five-cent Buffalo Wings." My son's grandmother hurried to the hostess stand, donned a white apron, and doled out chicken wings from a metal tray to big men wearing suspenders and holding dollars in their hands.

We shuffled out and gathered in the parking lot. No. 1 stepson had his black Volvo in idle. Tara helped Uncle Eli, Aunt Bella, Aunt Yonia, and Cousin Sharon into their car. Cousin Sharon wore a neck brace. She had been among several passengers hurt in a recent train derailment. Eight bags between the four of them were stuffed into the trunk, and Cousin Sharon sat up front. Tara helped her with the seatbelt because she couldn't get it on; lack of movement from her neck, I guess. Hugs, kisses, goodbyes. Ford trucks with people thirsty for "Dollar Buds" and "five-cent Wings" stormed the parking lot.

# Attic Addict

During the year after my mother passed away, Tara and I were extremely busy in California, holding down jobs, going to college, raising a son, and attending to all of life's day-to-day activities. There was little time to simply sit back and mourn. Thus, my mom's death hit me like a ton of bricks the following summer when we returned again to Cape May. This time I was back to sift through my mother's personal belongings. The Hubby decided to sell the Jefferson Street house and asked me to help clean it out. Particularly the attic, where there were numerous keepsakes, antiques, her old writings, personal diaries, newspaper clippings, correspondence, decades-old magazines, and numerous other items dating back to World War II. The task was not only painstaking; it was painful.

Tara and I spent endless hours going through old cartons and boxes. We cleaned and polished furniture, china, and silverware to auction off. Less expensive knick-knacks, dishes, pots and pans, books, and other items were prepared to be given away. Junk was piled outside the house and later taken to the dump.

Meanwhile, both of us had resumed work at the Cape May Beach Patrol as ocean lifeguards. Daytime I'd be life guarding. Nighttime I'd clean the house, which often required handling items that constantly reminded me of my tremendous loss. One of my beach patrol tasks was to teach a sixteen-year-old the rudiments of beach monitoring and ocean rescue. Sometimes I'd catch myself talking to her more about my woes than about keeping her eyes on the swimmers and blowing her whistle properly.

Each morning when I awoke, I felt ill at ease. Whether it was the workload, gloom over the loss of my mother, or something else, I wasn't sure. As it turned out, it was a little of both, plus something going seriously wrong inside my body. By the middle of the summer, I began having a constant dry cough. I wrote this off as allergies, or from working in the dusty attic. Every day, I'd climb up the worn wooden steps to that top floor, past an old metal fan. At the top was a large room, with a doorway to a huge second room. The first was filled with bookcases and miscellaneous furniture. It had served as a guest bedroom from time to time. Inside the second room was a virtual Smithsonian. Perfectly wrapped in wax paper were *Life* magazines, the covers of which pictured everything from President Kennedy's assassination to Astronaut Neil Armstrong walking on the moon. There were mementos from the 1939 New York World's Fair and books on unlocking your supernatural self. Plastic-covered formal dresses hung from the ceiling, including a bridal gown. Box after box contained letters to and from my mother's friends and lovers, rejection letters from publishers, and carbon copies of articles, stories, and poems my mother had written on her trusty typewriters.

> Some things you save forever. Not for all the king's horses and all the king's men would I part with certain scraps of paper, some tattered baby clothes and a few dog-eared dusty books. Say what you will about the worth of holding onto things when they are passe, but I will not change my mind. Someday someone will throw them away, but it won't be me.
> —"Joyride" II, December 19, 1979.

There were at least fifty diaries, which came as no surprise to me. She usually kept a diary at her bedside. In times of sadness or boredom, or following some exciting incident, she'd record everything from the day's weather to her most intimate thoughts. Once in a while, as a pre-teen boy, I'd be tempted to read those diaries. And I'd give in to that temptation. As an adult, I've become a firm believer in the sacredness of anyone's diary, just as I believe in not opening and reading someone else's mail. Still, she must have known someone someday would read them, and that it might be me. Now, rummaging through and cleaning the attic, I gave in to that temptation again. Her diaries were beautifully written. Not only did the words flow like she was writing for someone else, but her handwriting was downright artful. Her "L's" flowed like swirling clouds across the lined paper.

Both now and when I was a pre-teen, reading her diary made me uncomfortable. Of course, that's what I deserved. Certainly a twelve-year-old can't comprehend real depression, or what it's like to raise two children on income from work as a part-time legal assistant and freelance columnist.

"How come you keep a diary?" No. 2 asked me the other day.

"I just always have," I said.

"Can I read it?" he asked.

"In a word, no," I said.

"How come?" asked No. 2.

"Because it's personal," I said.

"What are you going to do with all your diaries?" asked No. 2.

"Burn them probably," I said.

"Burn them? Why?" he asked.

"I don't think the rest of the world is interested in me," I replied.

"When are you going to burn them?" asked No. 2. "When I'm very old and on my deathbed," I said.

"You might not be able to get up and burn them," said No. 2.

"That's a good point," I said. "I'll have to think about that."

—"Joyride" II, February 21, 1979

# Treasure Seekers

Relatives were starting to frequent the house and uncover some of the unknown treasures that were lost in the attic. One night, I was alone sneezing, coughing, and deliberating over what should be thrown out and what should be kept. I built a large pile of items, including old magazines, coffee tins (filled with trinkets such as old political buttons), and bookmarks from bookstores up and down the Eastern Seaboard.

In a sense, I enjoyed sitting amidst my mom's collectibles. Maybe I felt it would bring me closer to her in Heaven. However, for some reason, I always left the door to the attic open. I think it was to allow for a fast and easy escape.

One evening I left the house to buy some groceries at the local Acme supermarket. Mom had nicknamed this store "The Agony" because virtually every time she went there she met someone she knew who would talk her ear off, when all she wanted to do was buy a couple things and be out the door.

I came back from the store with two rolls, a tomato, a head of iceberg lettuce, and a block of New York cheddar. Every light in the house was on, even though I had turned out most of them before going to the store. I opened the screen door and entered, sensing immediately that someone else was in there with me. It couldn't be Tara. She was working at a restaurant up the street, and she wasn't scheduled to be home until a couple of hours later. My stepfather was away, working in Washington. Brother Keith was up in Philadelphia. "Hello?" I said in a loud voice. "Hello, anyone here?" Then came the sound of something falling, up in the attic. So I scrambled quickly up the three flights of stairs. As I passed the big-fan mid-point on the attic stairway, I saw her: Hunched over, wearing a long black coat, and carrying two canvas bags was Cousin Sharon. She had taken a bus from Philadelphia so she could go through some of my mom's things in the attic. "Why didn't you call?" I asked, annoyed.

"I did, the phone was always busy," she rebutted.

"Well, how long are you here for?" I asked.

"Just a couple of hours. I have to catch the 10:07 p.m. bus."

Sharon told me she had just come from a train convention in Atlantic City. Her bags were loaded down with pamphlets and literature about routes, transit technology, old locomotives, etc. Members of her family never seemed to travel without carrying two or three bags of who-knows-what. I glanced at my watch and saw that I would have exactly two hours of unbridled alone time with Cousin Sharon. She rummaged through my pile of forgotten memories and pulled out seven *Overeaters Anonymous* books. She put them in her bag. She then rambled on about how there was a book on paper dolls from the 1930s that Mom had promised her. She would not leave until she found it. Next, she pulled a crumpled piece of paper out of her pocket. It contained a wish list of Mom's belongings that Aunt Bella and Aunt Yonia wanted her to bring back on the bus. She inspected both rooms of cluttered junk, found my "throw-out pile," and put everything in it into one of her bags.

"Sharon, are you hungry?" I asked. I hoped I could lure her out of the attic and into the kitchen.

"No, I have a sandwich from this morning."

She pulled the sandwich out of her bag, from under several hard-back editions on overeating. Taking small bites out of it, she continued on her search for the paper doll book and the items on her mother's and aunt's wish lists. "You know, if you just leave me your list, when I get through everything, I'll put that stuff aside," I assured her.

"You'll forget," she declared.

"Oh no, I won't forget anything," I said.

"You forgot that I was coming today," she retorted.

"You said you called and the line was busy," I uttered.

"I called last week and left a message, too," she said, as she opened a book. "You know your mother's voice is still on the greeting on your answering machine?" she hastened to add.

"Yeah, I know, I just don't want to erase it," said I. "But that's beside the point. I didn't get your message."

Sharon is a professional volunteer. This means she doesn't get paid for her work. She's a secretary for the railroad commuter society, for instance. She also is a political activist for the local councilwoman. Sharon lives with her parents. They took care of her until she was in her mid-thirties. Then, as they became aged and infirm, the hierarchy reversed and she began taking care of them.

# Post Cards and Turkeys

Sharon's mother, my Aunt Bella, was a militant woman in her youth. My mother received from Aunt Bella, her elder sister, postcards crammed with writing. Her messages filled the usual allotted space, and then continued into every corner. Her writing twisted and turned to fill every available blank spot. My mom enjoyed reading them. Once, my mother turned the tables on my aunt. I recall her laughing hysterically as she wrote a postcard to Aunt Bella. She scribbled all over the postcard in tiny handwriting. Each word was barely discernable without a magnifying glass. She pranced around the living room, licked the stamp, and mailed the card to Philadelphia, figuring her sister would appreciate the joke. Weeks passed without a phone call or a post card from Aunt Bella. My mother ran to the mailbox every day in anticipation of her response. Then on a cloudy Monday, it arrived:

---

*Dear Libby,*

*That was the most amazing postcard I ever read. So much is happening in your life…*

*Bella*

---

My mom's oldest sister was unusual. Her household's holiday meals were a writer's dream. We traveled annually to her West Philadelphia row house for Thanksgiving dinner. Everything she cooked was bland. Spices and fancy cooking were not her fare. She boiled the turkey, overcooked the vegetables, and served pickled yams and canned Del Monte fruit cup for desert. One year, my mother declared, "Enough is enough. I'll cook the turkey." The night before that Thanksgiving Day, the sweet smell of turkey filled the air in our Cape May house. Soon we were bringing a new guest to Aunt Bella's for dinner—a precooked, twenty-pound turkey with all the trimmings.

During the two-hour drive to the city, the turkey was on my brother's and my mind. "How's the turkey? Is the turkey ok?" I'd ask. I was constantly concerned about the turkey's safety. "Mom, is the turkey wearing a seatbelt?"

She'd reply, "Yes, the turkey is fine."

My brother and I jointly carried the big turkey pan up Aunt Bella's porch steps. Each step was slow. Keith and I argued over who would walk backwards up the steps. My mother yelled directions to us the way a construction foreman might direct rookie crane operators: "Easy. Easy. Go a little to the left. Now the right."

> "Do you think a lot of families go through this at Thanksgiving?" asked No. 2.
>
> "I hope not," I said.
>
> I had offered to stuff and roast the turkey and bake two pumpkin pies for the family's dinner in the city.
>
> A few days before Thanksgiving, a telephone call came from the city. My sister said she'd rather have a raisin cake instead of the pumpkin pies.
>
> "I don't do raisin cakes," I said in a huff. "I do pumpkin pies."
>
> "Suit yourself," my sister said.
>
> "Besides," I said, "the pies are already baked."
>
> "I like raisin cake better," she said.

"Then go buy one," I said.
—"Joyride" II, December 1, 1982

When Aunt Bella opened the door she seemed delighted to see the new guest. She always gave us a big welcome, but never prepared her house for our visit. For instance, there usually was no place for us to sit. Old newspapers and other junk were stacked on virtually every chair in the house.

Maybe to prevent kids from locking themselves in the bathroom or other rooms, they had rubber bands on all the doorknobs. So the doors in the house never closed. When going to the bathroom, you had to nail your foot against the door to avoid potential embarrassment.

After years of carting the turkey up to the city, The Hubby suggested we eat out on Thanksgiving. "Yes, enough is enough," my mother again proclaimed. "We're eating out." So we again headed up to the city to have Thanksgiving dinner with my uncle, aunts, and cousin, but not at their house. Instead, we ate at a fine restaurant atop the elegant Hilton Tower hotel, which offered a buffet special for the holidays. My mother arranged for all of us to meet in the lobby. We took the elevator from there to the top floor, where we ate our fill. So satisfied was everyone that we never again ate a holiday meal at Aunt Bella's house. Every year, The Hubby, my mother, and my two aunts would search for another restaurant where we could eat Thanksgiving dinner.

We drove up from Cape May. Many times they were already eating when we arrived. Once they were approaching the buffet line for the second time. At the buffets, they'd go back for third and fourth helpings of certain items, notably desserts. After maybe their third or fourth trip to the buffet table, to my mother's horror, Aunt Bella would whip out plastic bags she had brought with her. In due course, gobs of cranberry sauce, mashed potatoes, turkey, meatballs, condiments, cake, pie, fruit, cookies, and so on went into the bags. My mother would softly yell, "Bella," to no avail. She went about her business like a traffic cop writing a ticket: focused, unapproachable, and steadfast. Cousin Sharon followed suit, and finally Uncle Eli grabbed a few items. After dinner they marched out, their bags bulging. We walked fifteen feet behind them.

# Canada Dry and Cape May

When my parents were living together, my mom told her mother and sisters she was going to move to the shore and write for a living. They believed such thinking was overly ambitious, idealistic, and a little bit selfish and stupid. She thought otherwise. So we moved.

I asked my mom how she decided to move to Cape May. She replied that, while we were living on Elfreths Alley in Philadelphia, she saw a Canada Dry commercial that featured Cape May. She and my father vacationed in Cape May several times. While there, the town seemed to her to be a good place to write and raise kids. So they looked for a house they could afford and found the one at 314 Jefferson Street. Looking out attic window, I imagined my mother seeing the house for the first time.

"Craig, Craig, Craig, are you listening?" Sharon asked. "Yeah, yeah. What time is it?" I replied. "When do I have to get you back to the bus station?"

I was carrying four bags full of miscellaneous books, a purple afghan, and the paper doll book she'd found under two pieces of rotting plywood. I drove Sharon to the bus stop with five minutes to spare and watched her board the bus to make sure she really left.

# Gladiators in the Morning

We went through the house item by item. Each day there seemed to be another request by someone for something that they thought was in the house. Some appeared to think that if they didn't get it, their life would be unbearable. No. 1 and his wife presented me with an itemized list of everything they wanted: tables, chairs, and family heirlooms like china and a bronze lamp with an eagle on it. At first I wanted nothing, and then I wanted everything. Everything around that house reminded me of Mom—from her rusting three-wheeled tricycle outside to the beat-up recliner chair that had the last newspaper she read stuffed into a pocket on its left side. The kitchen cabinets (and shelves in the attic) contained hundreds of dishes, glasses, and mementos, some still in their original boxes. My mother had bought many of these items at yard sales.

On Saturdays and Sundays she'd spend the morning hunting for treasures. Almost anything she saw could be a treasure in her eyes. She'd bring it back and find a place for it in the three-story warehouse we called home. She jammed, crammed, cluttered, and squeezed her treasures into the house any way she could.

She and her fellow "Early Birders" checked out yard sale sites very early. They would case the yard sale site first with a slow drive-by, back and forth. They'd watch their victims unloading boxes of goodies: old paintings, clothes, trunks full of green glassware. The "Early Birds" would send out a cryptic message to other "Early Birds" as to whether or not there was good stuff at the site. If they saw some good stuff, they'd line up on the sidewalk at promptly ten minutes before the sale started. Upon the sale's opening, a small frenzy would ensue. Like at an auction, my mother and her cronies would make ridiculous offers for items they knew deserved a higher price. She called it "low balling."

> My Saturday morning mission pits me against other Early Birds who go out seeking yard sales, searching for both trash and treasures. We lust for new, old, used and discarded objects with passionate equanimity; we enter the arena of yard sales as gladiators of the morning.
>
> If you step in front of me at the supermarket checkout, I won't say a thing. If you get ahead of me at the deli counter, well, then, so be it. But at a yard sale I'm no lady. When my eye lights on something, I'll push and shove my way through to get it first.
>
> Twenty or so years of "yard sailing" have honed my skills for the weekly melee. I have learned, for instance, to first scrutinize from the car; my jaundiced eyes quickly span the tables, and if something is sighted, I've got my running shoes on and I'm off.
> —"Joyride" III, June 29, 1994

Like boys who find rare comic books in basements of old houses, the Early Birds would gather their trophies and display them on wicker tables on my mother's porch. Usually, after hours of drinking tea, coffee and cold lemonade most of the women would come to the conclusion that everything they got wasn't worth keeping, though my mother would insist it was. They would leave empty-handed and my mother would stockpile everything that was gathered and put it away in her secret spots. I often wondered if she knew this would happen: that she would end up with all the yard-sale items the Early Birds had had so much fun seeking, examining, bargaining for, and then abandoning.

Returning to the itemized list that No. 1 son and his wife, Kris, prepared, I stood in my bare feet amidst the clutter of the attic. Tara gave a sly smile and said, "In honor of Libby we should have a yard sale." Not seeking any additional work, I said, "A yard sale? You must be kidding."

She wasn't. "Yes a grand yard sale," exclaimed Tara, as if she had just conceived a brilliant plan for a magnificent project. "Let's line the long driveway with card tables full of Libby's belongings and sell it back to the people she bought it from."

"Brilliant, a recycled yard sale bonanza," I commented.

Then she said: "Let's make a yard sale pile. We'll take almost everything now in our throw-out pile and put it into the yard sale pile. We need to do this for Libby."

I still wasn't sure. "You think so?" I asked.

"Think about it, Craig. It's irony at its finest," she explained. "Everything Libby elbowed and early-birded for is going to be elbowed and early-birded for again. Besides, this stuff probably is worth something because she kept it for so many years. What was junk then, 'yard sailors' now call antiques and collectibles."

> Anybody who's ever had a yard sale knows that you're only able to hold a few in a lifetime or you'll die from overexertion before your time. Yard sales are a lot of work: hauling things from attic and garage, sticking little labels on that usually end up sticking to you, and bargaining with people who won't pay more than a nickel for an item you have marked a dime.
> —"Joyride" II, July 28, 1976

While creating an ad to publicize our yard sale, I tried to recall the particular words Mom would look for when reading newspaper classified advertising sections, words such as: antiques, goodies, hard to find items, treasures, etc. She underlined and/or circled each buzzword in these ads in the *Cape May Star & Wave*, *Wildwood*

*Gazette-Leader*, and *Cape May County Herald* for possible "early birding." With my stepfather's and my wife's approval, I took it upon myself to write a stupendous classified ad that was bound to attract not only every yard sailor, but everybody in Cape May who could conceivably come to our yard sale.

News of the impending yard sale was already buzzing around town. Some of Libby's fellow Early Birds asked to come up to the attic and preview the stuff that was headed for the auction block. "No," I said.

"What do you mean 'No'?" demanded one Early Birder named Grace.

"I mean, 'No,'" I replied firmly.

"Why not?" she asked.

"Because Libby would want everything to be fair," I said.

"'Everything to be fair?'" she questioned.

"Yes, she'd want everything to be fair, just the way she played the game," I replied.

"'The game'?" she asked.

"The game," I said, happily.

"Craig, you're mistaken. At yard sales, Libby wasn't fair. She'd jump at the chance to preview yard sale stuff," she informed me.

I stood stupefied. "Uh, you think?" I mumbled.

"You aren't an Early Birder," she asserted.

I began to babble: "Err, no, I'm not. Umm, what's that matter? Err, uh, umm, she was my mother."

To which Grace exclaimed: "You don't understand the essence of early birding. Let me you tell something to enlighten you, boy: your mother was no yard sale angel."

I sat my butt on the edge of an old wooden table and wondered what would come from my mother's longtime friend next. Grace leaned on her right knee and spoke softly: "She was one of the most ruthless, diabolical Early Birds I've ever seen in my life. Don't think that your mother was the Mother Teresa of yard sailing. When it came to yard sales, she was bad."

It was as if someone had hit me on the head with a brick. For what seemed like a long time, I remained silent. Maybe she's right, I thought. Maybe my mother wasn't the saint I'd thought her to be. Maybe I should let Grace and her Early Birder cohorts preview the stuff. Oh, no. Just in time, I caught myself.

"Grace, you're still not getting into the attic," I exclaimed.

"So be it. You're a disgrace to your mother's Early Birder reputation," she pouted.

As she angrily walked out the door, I said, "Nice try; you almost had me there for awhile."

She couldn't have been too irate, because Grace showed up Saturday morning at ten of eight. As she rubbed her hands together in anticipation, she said, "I can't wait to see what your mother had."

The yard sale was a two-day extravaganza. Yard sailors like Grace stopped by the house throughout the week leading up to it. Thursday evening around six o'clock, a man who grinned peculiarly and held a cane knocked on the door. He introduced himself as Arnold, "an old friend of Libby's and a fellow yard sailor." As we shook hands, I asked, "Are you an Early Bird?"

To which he replied, "Oh, no, I'm outside that circle."

Circle? What circle? "What do you mean?" I asked him.

"I guess you could call me a friend of the Early Birds, but I'm certainly not one of them. I'm a collector," he said.

"A collector of what?" I asked.

"Frogs," he said.

"Frogs?" I responded.

"Frogs—porcelain, wooden, figurines, statuettes—frogs," he said.

In the laundry room of my mom's house, on two thin shelves over the sink, were frog statuettes. Maybe she kept them because our neighborhood was named Frog Hollow. It was so named because it has the lowest non-marsh land on the island. When I was very young, six or seven years old, those frogs intrigued me. I remember asking, "Where did these frogs come from?"

My mom's reply was, "They were bad kids who got turned into frogs because they wouldn't behave."

From then on, they were not high on my list of favorites. Actually, I didn't like them at all.

"Well, Arnold, you might be in luck. Libby has a frog collection," I said.

"I know," he replied, looking over my shoulder.

"How do you know about her collection?" I asked.

"She and her Early Birds arrived at a sale after the Windsor Mansion fire and she bought the whole box for two dollars," he said.

"The Windsor Mansion fire, that was almost fifteen years ago," I remarked.

"Yes, those frogs were a great find."

"I'll tell you what, Arnold, if you come back in an hour, I'll let you look at the frogs and any one you want, you can have," I said.

Arnold departed. I went to the laundry room and gathered all the frogs and put them into a cardboard box.

At exactly seven p.m., Arnold knocked on the door. "Hi, Arnold," I said.

"Hello," he replied.

I handed him the frogs. "How much do you want for them?" he asked.

"Nothing, they're yours," I said.

"I can't—please let me pay for them," he argued.

"Nope, Libby would want you to have them," I insisted.

"No she wouldn't," he corrected me. "She wouldn't? What do you mean?" I asked, shocked.

"She'd want me to pay for them," he said.

"Why?" I asked.

"Why? Because she was an Early Bird and Early Birds earned their worms," he remarked.

"Okay," I said laughingly. "How about a dollar for the whole box?"

"You got yourself a deal." Arnold pulled out a crisp dollar, handed it to me, and said, "Thank you."

He walked down the brick steps with his cane and his box of frogs. For me it was a learning experience, discovering that every club, even an informal one such as the Early Birds, has its rules, and that even would-be members take them very seriously.

# Yard Sale Bonanza

Up at six in the morning on Saturday, I found Tara already bringing stuff down from the attic. My stepbrother Johnny and his wife Nancy had come down Friday night to help out with the big sale. I carried every table that was up in the attic down three flights of stairs and lined them up along the driveway. Early Birds were casing the house as the family placed items on the tables. Slow-moving vehicles—Pintos, Mavericks, and Novas—made numerous loops around the block. Yes, they even had the audacity to enter the driveway before eight o'clock.

"No Early Birds," I bellowed at the top of my lungs through the third-story attic window.

A gathering of four people—three women in their mid-fifties and one man in his sixties—scurried away like mice from a wheel of cheese. At seven forty-five a.m., a line was starting to form at the head of the driveway.

"Craig, you better get out here," Tara yelled nervously from the driveway.

"What's going on?" I hollered down from the attic.

"There's a lot of people down here. We should just let them in," Tara said.

"No. Absolutely not. Not until eight o'clock, and that's final," I vehemently shouted.

"You heard it, people," Tara barked at the gathering crowd.

My stepbrother's wife, Nancy, prepared her money belt, counting out dollar bills and change, while my stepbrother and I carried the big items down the steps.

Tara kept time. "Two minutes to eight. You need to get down here, Craig—now," she commanded.

As I ran down the steps, I saw more than a hundred people lined up along the sidewalk: women, children, collectors, Early Birds, bed and breakfast owners. Some carried baskets, some shopping bags, one even had a wheelbarrow.

"Okay, people, this is a two-day sale; different stuff on both days," I loudly announced. "No pushing or shoving. Prices are negotiable. Good luck. The sale has—begun."

There was a rush of people. Sweat poured down my face as I witnessed yard selling at its finest. I'm sure Libby was laughing out loud, wherever she was, watching Arnold, Grace, and their fellow yard sailors battling it out in the trenches. After about an hour of haggling over prices for paintings, chairs, blenders, and everything else my mother held sacred, the mob mellowed. By two p.m., only stragglers remained. Families on their way to the beach stopped to buy plastic sand toys my brother and I had played with years before. There were cigar boxes that could hold trinkets, and *Reader's Digest*s to page through while on the beach. By four p.m., Tara and I carried the big tables to the backyard and put leftover items on them. We placed blue plastic tarps over the tables and started gathering more stuff for the next day's yard sale.

Sunday's sale was no different. Word got around Saturday night that new stuff would be sold on the following day. Everyone at Saturday's sale appeared again on Sunday. Joining them were newcomer bargain hunters.

We brought in over $1,200 in two days and were exhausted.

# Changing Season

As colder weather approached, we continued to clear out Mom's house, periodically arguing with No. 1 and his wife that they should help us more. My stepfather had moved out, and the house was up for sale. Tara and I prepared to bring back a truckload of household items and other stuff we had saved for ourselves. No. 1 told me there shouldn't have been so much work because I should have sold whatever I could and thrown everything else away. Except for a few items he kept, my brother wanted us to get rid of it all. Just the opposite, I couldn't bear to part with anything. We had sold some antiques and bric-a-brac to dealers and collectors, and there was the stuff we had sold at the yard sales. Weeks before, The Hubby had moved his office and bedroom items to his new residence up north. The remaining furniture, cartons, keepsakes, etc., we loaded into a fifteen-foot U-haul truck. By the time we finished, it was packed like a sardine can.

> It is hard to say goodbye. I have said goodbye to people, to houses, to childhood and to childhood dreams.
> —"Joyride" III, February 26, 1997

We started our long journey back to the West Coast on a cold October day, 12 months and 1 day after the death of my mother. Tara and I each drove a vehicle, using two-way radios to keep in contact. We took turns driving the fifteen-foot U-Haul van and our Isuzu Trooper. As we drove, each day I began to feel worse and worse. The dry cough persisted. I downed Sudafed every six hours, but the cough just worsened.

Every morning I awoke feeling lousy. At first, I thought it was gloom from the loss of my mom. Then I began to suspect it might be something physical. One morning, shortly after waking, I felt a lump next to my clavicle. I started to freak. Maybe it was a pulled muscle, I thought, although no pulled muscle I'd had ever felt like this. I took my index finger and caressed the round edge of my left shoulder, slowly moving down toward my chest. My middle finger held steady on a foreign object that felt like a rubber ball. I fondled it constantly, monitoring it to see if it got bigger or smaller.

Across the country we drove, sixteen hours at a time. Driving that length of time can cause your mind to wander to hell and back. I was tripping out. Worse case scenarios flashed through my brain. Me in a hospital bed, whispering my final words. Tara, crying a flood of tears. My son, head bowed, hiding his eyes behind his little hands in grief.

We reached San Luis Obispo, in central California. My mom's best friend of fifty years lived there with her husband. Always very kind to us, they'd invited us to stop by anytime. So we did. Ann and Ron were happy to see us. We had visited them before, but this was the first time since my mom's death. Though silver haired, Ann seemed much younger than her age, thanks to an active life, including aerobic classes with other sixty-somethings. Ron's rugged countenance and lumberjack shirt reminded me of the actor Clint Eastwood. Their guestroom was ready for our arrival, with fresh sheets, open windows, and curtains rustling from a sea breeze.

# Trick or Treat

When I awoke at eleven o'clock the next morning, I felt so terrible I decided I needed to see a doctor. Dragging myself out to the porch, where Tara, Ron, and Ann were drinking coffee, I asked, "Where is the closest doctor?"

Ann said, "What's the matter, Craig? Are you feeling okay?"

"No," I replied, "I feel terrible, and there's this lump below my shoulder that shouldn't be there."

It was Sunday, but fortunately there was a "doc in the box" around the corner that was open. As I entered the "doc in the box," I knew something was wrong inside my body. Sweat poured from my palms. My feet felt heavy. My neck ached. Suddenly, the walls of the building seemed to melt away.

The doctor saw me right away. As if dressed for a Halloween cruise in the South Pacific, he wore a Hawaiian print shirt showing a couple on a beach watching a sunset. His pants were vacation white. Likely in his mid-forties, he enthusiastically asked, "What's up?" and I told him about the lump and the dry cough. I also said my ears were all clogged up, probably from surfing and swimming. I wondered if maybe all these symptoms were connected. He walked behind me as I sat on a metal table with both feet dangling. With his left hand, he quickly pushed against the lump next to my clavicle.

"No, your clogged ears are the least of your problems," he stated.

"What do you mean?" I asked, fearing the worst.

While squeezing my lump firmly with his index and middle finger he said slowly, "Well, I think you either have tuberculosis, AIDS, or cancer."

"What? You've got to be kidding." This had to be some cruel Halloween joke, I thought. "You're joking, aren't you?" I asked.

"No," he declared solemnly. "I'm sorry. You need to see a doctor immediately when you get home."

I threw my shirt across the room and kicked the wall repeatedly. Alternately swearing and crying, I calmed down only after Tara grabbed and hugged me. "This guy's a quack," I told her. "Only a quack would say what he said after such a quick examination. How can he say I have cancer, AIDS, or tuberculosis? What the hell does he know? He's just somebody who works in a 'doc in the box,' for crap's sake. I need to talk to his boss. Where's his supervisor?"

The "doc in the box" nurse overheard my rant and upbraided me: "He is the supervisor. He owns the clinic. If you don't like his diagnosis, go see someone else, but you have no right to be yelling like that and using such foul language."

"Yelling? Foul language? Do you know what he just told me? He just told me I'm practically going to die," I snapped back.

"He didn't tell you were going to die," she said, in a tone of admonition.

"What the hell good does it do me to hear this garbage? It can't be true. What the…?"

"Calm down," she interrupted.

"Calm down. You calm down," I shot back.

"The doctor isn't going to charge you for your visit," the nurse said, in a more genial voice. "And I'm willing to clean your ears for free also."

"Clean my ears. What good is that if I'm going to die?" I sighed sadly.

"I told you, nobody said you're going to die. Now do you want your ears cleaned or what?" she softly half-demanded.

"Yeah, I suppose so," I said, breathing a deep sigh.

She took out a syringe without a needle and flushed warm water and alcohol into my ear. Big black pieces of wax filled the ear basin she was holding. Fine pebbles of sand and other assorted beach properties went into the tub. "How does that feel?"

"Better…thanks," I said.

"You're welcome. Now hang in there; things will work out," she stated calmly.

I walked with Tara out into the lobby, a bit calmer. We approached the desk and the receptionist confirmed that "The doctor is not going to charge you for your visit."

On the way from the Halloween-decorated clinic to Ann and Ron's place, breathing was difficult. Every murmur, every word, every motion the doctor had made was imprinted in my mind. What was to come next? Was I destined to live a life of disease like my mother? Ann and Ron were completely blown away when they heard the diagnosis. Tara was in shock. She hardly said a word. I was frantic inside. I wanted out of San Luis Obispo immediately. I wanted to be back in Santa Cruz.

A close friend, Sterling, an ER doctor, often was helpful when I had a health question. Once I'd called him and asked if he could come over and check out what felt like a small pebble in my throat. It was Friday night and he was about to go into work for an eight-hour shift. He was at my house. After a quick examination of my throat and neck, he said, "Worry about something else."

# The "C" Word

I called Sterling on arrival in Santa Cruz, leaving message after message on his home phone and beeper. I even called him at work and found out from a nurse he was on a surfing trip in Mexico. Two days later I saw him riding his bike along the beach accompanied by two young women bicyclists. I ran up to him and said, "Sterling. Hey, Sterling. I've been trying to call you. I want you to look at something. Please, I'm freaking out. I need help. Please." He pulled his bike over to the sidewalk. "Will you feel this lump I have?"

He looked at it. Man, if that wasn't pitiful, I don't know what was. Here I am with my shirt off asking a doctor who is obviously enjoying himself in the company of two beautiful women to drop everything and check me out. Here I am saying, "Um, excuse me, will you feel this lump I have?" How pitiful is that?

Sterling assured me it probably wasn't anything serious. He advised me not to worry about it. On the following day, though, he called and asked me to go to the hospital for a chest x-ray. Just to be safe, he said. Hmmm, I thought, he must suspect something bad, maybe some deadly disease. I went. Waiting for the results was unnerving. You can die a thousand times in your mind when you're waiting for test results on your health. Three days after the x-ray, Sterling called me and said, "Craig, I'm not going to beat around the bush; I'm just gonna give it you straight."

My heart pounded wildly. "Well give it to me," I said.

"I think you have Hodgkin's disease," he confided.

"What's that?" I asked.

"Cancer."

The dreaded C-word. Death. I was going to die. It had come to this. I had survived my mom's suffering and death, a paddle in hurricane seas, an impossible sandwich shop business, and now…How could God do this to me?

"Is this bad?" I asked Sterling.

"It's manageable," he replied.

"What does that mean 'manageable'? Give me some answers," I pleaded.

"I don't have a lot of answers. This isn't my specialty."

Tears poured from my eyes. My face was hot. My head was hot. I wanted to run, paddle, leave my body. This time there was no way to escape. I couldn't escape from my own body.

"I called a friend who's an oncologist and she'd be glad to see you and answer any questions you have." He told me her phone number as I shook.

I hung up the phone and told Tara that Sterling thought I had cancer. She stepped back and looked into my eyes and said, "We can handle this."

When I received the bad news, we were taking refuge at Tara's parents' house in the valley. It was hot and there was no breeze. "I want out of here," I said.

"Where do you want to go?" she asked.

"Back to Santa Cruz."

Tara called the number I had scribbled onto some paper. She spoke to the secretary of the physician Sterling had recommended. She couldn't give me an appointment. "She said she isn't taking on any new patients," Tara told me.

"What? Sterling said she would see me. Did you tell her that?" I said.

"Yeah, but I didn't talk to the doctor, just the secretary."

"Let's go," I said.

"Where?" asked Tara.

"To her office," I said.

"Now?" she asked.

"Yeah, now," I declared.

We sped toward Santa Cruz for two hours and arrived in the afternoon. My thoughts were scattered and calculating in the same instant. Then came a revelation: maybe all this was happening for some worthwhile higher purpose. Maybe I was destined to experience and appreciate some of what my mom went through. I was to be her shadow, so to speak. Doctors, hospitals, x-rays, blood tests, nurses, needles, etc., were these to be my fate, too? My future was all too clear; yet very foggy, too.

Moments after Tara parked, I ran into the doctor's office. It was crowded with patients and looked more like a lounge room in a hotel than an oncologist's office. People were spread on couches and recliners. They were drinking coffee and eating cheese pastries. Behind a counter was a dark-skinned woman whose long black hair hung down to her hips. "May I help you?" she inquired. She didn't seem to notice that I looked like a madman—clearly frazzled, bug eyed, pale skinned, coffee-stained shirt, and nervously shivering.

"I'm here to see the doctor," I said.

"Do you have an appointment?" she asked.

"No, I just need to see her," I shot back, clenching my fists.

"She's seeing a patient," she said, as if she was talking to a delivery boy or pharmaceutical salesman.

"I have to see her. When will she be done?" I said, in a pleading, almost begging tone.

"This is her last patient," she said sternly.

I waited outside on a chair next to her door. After fifteen minutes she came out. "Hi," I said.

"Hi," she said.

"I'm Craig, Sterling's friend," I said.

"Yes, come on in and we'll talk."

Sitting, she picked up the x-ray film and waved me toward a chair. "I've already reviewed your x-rays," she said.

"And?" I asked.

"I think you have Hodgkin's," she said.

"And?" I asked.

"And—we have to stage it and figure out how far the cancer has progressed." She anticipated my next question: "Do I think you're going to die from this? I don't think so—but we need to find what stage you're at."

She noticed my shakes and shivers. She detected I was hanging on her every word. She recognized that I was bewildered, depressed, afraid, and desperately seeking some answers. Tara held my hand softly as the doctor spoke words like "biopsy," "metastasized," and "chemotherapy." It was a horrible dream and I wanted to wake up and find it was just a nightmare caused by indigestion.

# No Worries, Mate

Next came a wave of guilt. Had I brought this dreadful disease on myself? Had I worried myself sick? The next few nights, I stayed up worrying about all the worrying I'd done in the past. I worried that my worrying probably caused the cancer that would now bring my sudden death. Worse, it would be a long and painful death. My constant worrying about losing my mom was the reason I was sick, I began to think.

> We are never without our worries, big and small, from the time we leave the cradle. Maybe even before.
> I certainly could qualify for the Worry Award of the Year because there is not a moment of the day that goes by that I can't think of a good reason to worry.
> I spend nights turning and tossing, reliving the day's events, worrying about the next day, worrying about next week, next month, the next decade. You have no idea how broad a range my worries encompass....
> —"Joyride" II, October 13, 1975

A week went by and I heard nothing from anyone. It was nearing Thanksgiving and the weather was changing. So was my state of mind. Once a person who almost never worried about anything, I began worrying constantly. From someone who previously had no trouble falling asleep, I turned into an insomniac, staying up all night worrying. I was a mess. In the daytime, I tried to fill my hollow feeling of anxiety with surfing. I surfed like crazy. I really didn't feel all that bad physically. I had a constant cough, but I could manage that. What I couldn't manage was the nagging mental anguish I was suffering.

I finally heard back from my doctor. She said: "You're in stage II, which means you need to have chemo. There's a great chance you will have a full recovery. But the chemo will be difficult. You'll have to go through twelve weeks of it, then six weeks of radiation. We want to burn this shit out of you. I'm not taking any chances."

It was as if she was speaking a foreign language. I heard the words, and recognized some of them, but didn't quite comprehend what she was really saying.

The scheduled date of my first chemo session was the Monday after Thanksgiving. I had exactly three weeks and four days until the needle. An old friend from Fort Lauderdale, Florida, flew in for some surfing and hanging out. I told him my sad tale. I told him I was going to surf hard every day until that fateful Monday arrived. We traveled up and down Highway 1 looking for waves. We surfed in Ocean Beach in San Francisco, Ano Nuevo outside Santa Cruz, and every other spot that had even a hint of some good waves. In a way, I felt like the guy in the Jerry Lewis movie, *Hook, Line, & Sinker*, who was told he was going to die and decided he'd do anything he wanted. He spent his life savings parachuting out of airplanes, eating filet mignon at the finest restaurants, taking all kinds of crazy risks, and spending a week on an exotic island drinking Mai-Tai's from coconut shells during the daytime and fire dancing at night.

# *Armageddon*

Sunday night, before my first treatment, we stayed up watching the movie "Armageddon." A meteorite was en route to destroying the earth and the only thing that could stop it was a band of misfit oil drillers. As I watched, I gobbled peanut butter. An article on the Internet I read said that chemo patients should watch their weight. So, there I was, rebelliously eating gobs of fatty peanut butter. Halfway through the movie, Bruce Willis' character said goodbye to his movie daughter before going into space to drill the asteroid to pieces. He hugged her. She cried. He cried. I cried, into my jar of peanut butter. I'm pitiful, I thought. "Snap out of it," I told myself, walking to the bathroom to wash off the peanut butter and anxiety.

The first few chemotherapy treatments didn't bother me physically. Though I initially pretended to be a superman that chemo couldn't weaken, the doses started to take their toll. After all, even the comic book Superman was weakened by a mysterious material named kryptonite.

One day, while Tara was at work and my son was at school, I lay on the couch bloated from the Prednisone prescribed by the doctor to prevent any infections. Sick to my stomach, I turned on the TV looking for something to take my mind off my current condition. I watched two movies in a row, *The Karate Kid* and *Rocky*. The first ends up with a teenage Karate Kid clobbering a bully who harassed him throughout the entire movie. In the second, South Philly prizefighter Rocky Balboa wins the world's boxing championship, knocking out one opponent after another. The TV station promoted the pair as "Fight Movies for Guys" time. After watching four hours of violent fight movies, I was in a fighting mood, all fired up to whip my own worthy opponent—cancer.

# Confucius Say

Alternative medicine fascinated me even before I was sick. I've always thought acupuncture, herb medications, and Asian philosophy have curative powers. So I welcomed the acupuncture sessions that began on the first day of my chemotherapy treatments. I went to a Chinese acupuncturist named Joanna Zaho. She had a very calming presence, listening first, speaking later. She was humble but confident. Her skin was light brown and her hands were thin. She walked slowly and never took her eyes away from mine. After Tara and I sat down and explained my condition, we told her that I would be receiving chemotherapy for twelve weeks and that every third week would bring a double treatment.

The acupuncturist insisted I receive acupuncture before and after the chemo. This had both physical and mental benefits, as it offset the side effects of the chemotherapy. These included constipation, diarrhea, uncontrollable bloody noses, and pain in all my joints.

As the doses increased, the doctors questioned my immune system's ability to handle the stress. I became concerned about this myself when, one February morning, I awakened feeling unusually hot and sore. During the treatments, I always woke up feeling crappy, but this time I felt more crappy than usual. After I paged my doctor and she called back, I told her I felt really feverish and that my body felt very sore all over. She instructed me to come to her office.

I was a wreck by the time I entered the lobby. Tears fell down my cheeks nonstop. My composure had disappeared. Things were starting to go really bad. She took my temperature. It was one hundred and three degrees. She administered antibiotics and said that if my temperature rose, I should check myself into the emergency room.

I went home sobbing and Tara suggested that maybe Dr. Zaho, the acupuncturist, could do something for me. A little over two hours later, I was in her office telling her about my high fever and body soreness. She started treatment immediately. My temperature began to drop. I began to feel better. I went home actually feeling much better. It was amazing. Along with acupuncture, I took Chinese herbs to alleviate my nausea. The herb tea tasted horrible but really helped calm my stomach.

Chi Gong is a Chinese breathing method. Sometimes called "vital energy brain control," it can be used to help manage and prevent disease, as well as maintain good health. For a while, I drove to a hilltop Buddhist retreat to attend Chi Gong classes. Breathing and sudden movements of the body, along with concentration, were among the exercises taught there. I became calm after I started practicing Chi Gong.

# *Surf's Up*

As the chemotherapy took its toll, I surfed in my mind but not in the water. I exercised when going through chemo, but I wasn't even thirty percent of my regular self. The heavier the doses of chemo, the weaker I got. Swells were hitting the coastline daily. When January and February arrived, the waves came in droves. My favorite time of the year was happening without me. I woke up in the morning and walked my overweight dog to the oceanfront. Surfers littered the water, and rarely did a wave go by without someone on it.

During the second month, I received chemo treatment on two consecutive days back to back once a week. In the treatment room, some patients had books, magazines, crossword puzzles, loved ones. IV bags dripped colors of red and white into the willing and unwilling alike. Some watched each drip slowly travel down the plastic tube into their veins. Some kept glancing at the clock. Some seemed absorbed in conversation and unaware of the clock. I did everything: watched the clock, watched the drip, watched the patients, the nurses, the loved ones, the faces, and the moods.

Three hours later, I was at the cliff checking the surf. My surfboard and wetsuit were in the back of my truck. It was low tide and the wind was howling offshore. Conditions were perfect. I saw six guys out there. The waves were about eight feet and barreling top to bottom. They were jacking up on the shallow part of the reef and forming a perfect tube. My blood was hot and pumping. I wasn't sure if I was hot from the medicine I'd just received, or because I was scared of going out there into the ocean. I've been surfing for over twenty years—and a day like this is challenging to a surfer even when he is in the best of health. Now, with medicine pumping through my bloodstream, and in a debilitated state, I was foolishly getting ready to go out into the waves.

I walked back to the truck and took off my shirt. Friends of mine walked by, giving me a thumbs-up sign as they peered at my bald head. I tore the white tape off my right arm that kept the cotton ball in place over my vein. I could hear Mom's voice in my head. "Mom's out there, she wants me out there, and I need to be out there," I said to myself. I slowly put my wetsuit on and carried my board down to the beach. I stretched on the sand and watched the waves grow and the tide lower. Guys were going left on the wave and getting launched into oblivion. I paddled out slowly, letting each hand glide through the water. The water was colder than the usual fifty-five degrees.

I had no business being out there. I paddled all the way out and floated among the guys I used to battle for the set waves. Today I wanted nothing to do with the mean ones. Maybe I'll just sit out here, I thought. I was shivering although I had only been out there for a few minutes. Then the horizon changed. Everyone started to move out to sea. There was a set of waves. They were coming—and big. My initial feeling was to paddle in, but instead I stroked hard. Three waves crashed over my head. When I turned around to sit up on my board, I noticed there was no one around. They'd been washed in. Everyone was cleaned up. Somehow I weaseled through that massive set. Don't ask me how. Maybe "Mother Ocean" was looking out for me.

Minutes later, a stronger set of waves appeared on the horizon. I turned around and paddled for a wave. I took two hard strokes and slowly got to my feet. The takeoff was slow. As my board made it halfway down the face, the wave got extremely hollow as it hit the inside of the reef's north side. Another ledge of the wave appeared and a double-up effect happened quickly. I air-dropped into the second part of the wave and inserted myself into a long hollow tube that closed in around my frail figure. My right hand gently felt its way through the inside of the lip, and seconds later I was spit out from the force of the wave compressing. I coasted out of the wave, amazed that I wasn't dreaming. I needed that moment in time. Although that was my only wave of the session, it boosted my confidence. It brought me a step closer to ushering in a new relationship with my mother, in a playground so familiar to the both of us.

# *Warrior Mode*

I started to get into the habit of wearing green army pants on the days I would receive my treatment. As I put them on, they felt empowering. In a sense, I felt I was going to war. *I'm a warrior.* My head was shaved. My weight was up from the steroids. And I felt aggressive toward my present condition. I was going to kick some fucking ass. I was going to put this cancer in a full nelson and squeeze so hard that it would beg for me to let it go.

> Whoever said "Life is a game" was right on the mark.... Sometimes a friend will drop by on a Sunday afternoon and find me watching [a football game on television] and is stunned to find me growling and cheering.
>
> Frankly I never encouraged No. 1 and No. 2 sons to play football during their growing years—too rough for my nervous system. But now that I'm older and wiser, I now understand the underlying psychology of following a team.
>
> We rise and fall with their every move. We put our faith in their efforts and, for two hours or so, we forget everything.
>
> We love to win. We hate to lose.
>
> We can be knocked down, tackled, bloodied and land at the bottom of a heap of bruisers out to make us hit the ground.
>
> But we learn to get up and dust ourselves off, and come back to fight on.
>
> I understand this better than ever nowadays.
> —"Joyride" III, September 10, 1997

After one of my last chemo treatments, my doctor called me at home. She told me about this seventeen-year-old girl who was diagnosed with the same cancer I had. Like every patient, she was having a rough time with chemo. My doctor wanted to know if I could give the girl some words of encouragement and tell her what to expect. After a few days, I decided to give the girl a call. She answered after the first ring and sounded very young and scared. I told her that my doctor gave me her number and suggested I call, given that I had been diagnosed with the same disease, in the same phase, and gone through the same treatment. I assured her that I was fine. Although feeling somewhat rundown, I told her I was very optimistic about the future. She expressed disappointment and disgust about being bald and bloated. She told me she was an aspiring model and she couldn't stand to look at herself in the mirror. She said, "My bald head is a constant reminder of my cancer." I then told her she needed to get into "warrior mode," and that warriors shave their heads, gain extra pounds, and get ready for the big heavyweight battles. She started to cry. She apparently did not like my pep talk. Instead, she just answered automatically, as if she had stopped listening: "Yeah, ok, yeah, ok, uh huh." I wound down the conversation and told her that I would come visit her surrounding her next chemo treatment.

The Tuesday after our conversation, I rode my bike to the treatment center. When I saw her, she had on a Walkman and was wearing sunglasses. Her legs were sprawled out on her mother's lap, with a blanket over them. An IV was in her arm. She hardly acknowledged me. I sat there through most of her treatment conversing with her mother. Before I was about to leave, the girl tugged on my T-shirt and told me that she didn't like the conversation that we had on the telephone. She said that it made her upset. She said she was not prepared to hear that it was going to be a "fight." I apologized but told her that, unfortunately, if she was going to enter the arena she needed to know it was not going to be a fashion show. She smiled and put the earphones back on. Her mom thanked me for coming.

# *Water World*

While undergoing treatment, I took hot showers for long periods of time. In fact, showering became an obsession. Sometimes I'd take twenty showers a day. Sometimes they would last thirty minutes. If you do the arithmetic, it might seem ridiculous, but my obsession was driven by an intense focus on meditation. I liked to feel the water streaming and pounding on my neck and body. I could hear nothing but the water hitting my head and falling into the tub. The steam from the hot water made the bathroom feel dreamy. I remember trying every different position in the shower. I would try lotus, then go to prone position, then fetal, and then eventually lie down completely, letting the water hit my chest. I became very disappointed when the water heater started to shut down and the shower spurt out lukewarm water. I would abruptly shut off the shower and hope the water would warm up soon, so I could be back in my Water World of comfort and serenity.

# You'll Be Okay, Kid

My chemotherapy treatment was scheduled to end in the middle of March. Then I'd undergo six weeks of radiation. I had a few weeks to get my body back in order before the first week in May, when my radiation treatment started. I sat with the doctor who was overseeing my doses weeks later. He told me how he was from Long Beach Island, New York, where he used to body surf. That made me feel good; maybe he'd understand my connection with the ocean. He spun around on his leather chair behind his desk and said, "They'll take good care of you, kid. You don't have to worry about anything." One of my mother's pet peeves was medical staff who would condescendingly assure her, "You'll be okay," without considering all the factors: the medicine, her condition, etc.

I started radiation therapy on a Monday. The first treatment consisted of a measurement of four standard dots (tattoos) on my chest to line up where the bulk of radiation would be. Those dots are always there on my chest. Like little targets, they marked where the radiation rays would be concentrated. Tuesday was a bit more challenging. With my shirt off, I lay on a cold table with my head kept perfectly still via a face harness resembling a medieval torture chamber item or a vicious dog's muzzle. This was strapped around my face, securing my head against the table. I told the technicians, "Get this thing off me. I can't handle this."

A young man in his twenties insisted, "This is standard stuff, man. You have to wear it."

In a muffled voice (because I couldn't move my mouth) I protested, "I don't care; I feel like an animal. I can't wear this."

"You have to," he said.

"No I don't," I said.

"Yes you do."

"I'll tell you what, you might as well leave this thing on me because if this thing comes off, I'm going to kick your butt," I said angrily.

"Mary, Mary, Mary," he yelled.

"Who is Mary?" I asked.

"She's the supervisor," he replied in a shaky voice.

The lights in my eyes and the glistening ceiling were slowly killing me. I needed out. There I was under the thumb of some twenty-something and his supervisor. I was so vulnerable, just like mom had been. I finally understood that when you're sick, you're a baby, a dog, anything but independent. I'd never fully understood my mother's words about how she was treated as a patient. I was too consumed with being depressed about my own situation that I never took in her point of view, her real feelings. Sure, I listened and thought for a brief moment, but how she really felt had never registered.

There was no way of getting around the face harness. Like Jesus with his crucifix, for the time being, I was attached to this face harness. I wore it for five more weeks.

Although the mental anguish of wearing the harness wore me down, my body was feeling stronger and starting to recover from the powerful medicine pumped into my veins. Spring was in the air. With the blossoming of flowers came the blossoming of a new life, one without cancer growing inside of me.

# The Attic: Scary Place

When I was a little boy, the attic seemed like a scary place. In boxes, I would find aging paperbacks on the supernatural. Apparently, my mom wanted to tap into a higher power, or at least learn something about paranormal matters. One Christmas Eve, as I lifted a small box of tree ornaments, I noticed, out of the corner of my eye, a Ouija board. Suddenly, strange noises and flashing lights came through the attic's small half-moon-shaped windows. It scared the crap out of me.

Boxes were stacked one atop the other. As we lifted and moved the boxes, we heard bumps and thumps, "obviously" from us moving them. That wasn't obvious to me, however. It was pretty dark and No. 1 son was sometimes hidden from my view behind piled-up cartons and other obstacles. I thought a ghost had made the noises. No. 1 later named this ghost "Fred." We decided Fred was "a good ghost because he only came at Christmas time." My mom told me Fred probably was a "good spirit" and that he materialized because there was so much joy and love in the air.

Even though I thought Fred probably was good, I became petrified when she told me to go up the attic stairs and click on the light, so that we could bring down more boxes labeled "Xmas decorations." Christmas came and went, and so did Fred.

Maybe my mother wanted to learn how to become a witch, so that she could turn me into a frog when I misbehaved. Maybe she was, like most of us at one time or another, searching for the meaning of life, investigating levels of existence far beyond what we can see, hear, smell, and touch. It's obvious to me now that my mother was definitely in tune with something spiritual.

> "Well, what could I do?" I said. "I had no choice. There was no room for it in my suitcases."
>
> "You go on a trip and come back walking through the airport wearing a witch's hat," said No. 2.
>
> "I thought it would be fun for Halloween," I said. "I knew I'd be busy once I got home and probably wouldn't be able to come up with a Halloween costume in a hurry. I never even gave it a second thought that it wouldn't fit into my baggage.
>
> "It was only a hat. At least I didn't come off the plane carrying a broom too," I said.
>
> —"Joyride" III, November 6, 1985

# Mysterious Boy

On a chilly October night when I was eight years old, she told me that she was in the kitchen boiling water when a silhouette of a small boy approached the back door of the kitchen. She told me that when she saw it, she wasn't scared. She said she moved closer to investigate and talked with him. She asked him what he wanted, and he told her he needed help. She said the boy appeared to be around nine or ten years old. His face was hard to make out. He stood at the door and talked with her for over five minutes, she said. When she looked away for a moment, he simply disappeared. Apparently, at that time, my brother and I were sleeping.

She told The Hubby what happened and asked him to drive her someplace in his car. She didn't know where exactly. She wanted to find this mysterious boy. After checking to see that her sons were fast asleep, they drove toward the beach, then up and down Beach Drive, slowing down at each blinking traffic light. At the end of Beach Drive, they saw other off-and-on lights. They weren't traffic lights, but the flashing lamps atop police cars and ambulances. The Hubby stopped the car, thinking that maybe this was what the kid at the back door was talking about.

Rescue workers were scattered about on the small stretch of beach. Mom tied the strings of her jacket's hood and followed her husband, surveying the scene. Mom approached a police officer holding a flashlight. "What's going on?" she asked.

Pointing toward the ocean, the officer replied, "There is a small sailboat out there that's in trouble. We can't reach it by radio, so we're trying to guide them into port using searchlights."

She asked if he knew who was on the boat.

"I heard it's a family sailing to Florida."

Mom and The Hubby sat on a boardwalk bench. They watched the police shine beacons of light toward the small sailing craft, as a Coast Guard cutter came speeding to the rescue. "They'll be safe now; there's nothing more for us to do," Mom said to The Hubby.

They got up from the bench and returned to the car. Later, The Hubby told me the whole incident was really spooky. He wondered if my mom really had talked with a boy-like spirit who went from house to house seeking help for the people on the boat.

The next day, the front page of the *Atlantic City Press* ran a story about the Coast Guard rescue of a family on a sailboat that got lost in a windstorm. It had been en route from Ventnor, New Jersey, to Florida. The owner, lacking sailing experience, had bought the boat just a few weeks before. After he lost his bearings, the boat's radio conked out. In the boat with him was his nine-year-old son.

That incident intrigued me for years. From then on, I assumed my mother was sometimes on a different playing field than the rest of us mortals. I always thought she was intuitive, but after that she became more of an enigma to me. Sometimes I'd watch her as she thought intently about something, maybe for a future column, or how she was going to make the house mortgage payment. Her eyes focused on nothing in particular and I wondered if she was somehow channeling spirits.

I read her diaries and her books on the supernatural. I sought to discover her attachment to the paranormal. Maybe, I thought, I'll unlock something that will reveal her secret spirituality. I fantasized about my mother maybe stirring a huge vat of bubbling brew and sticking needles into a scruffy doll that resembled the Ayatollah.

Maybe, I thought, they weren't school board meetings she was at until ten o'clock at night. Maybe she was at secret pagan rituals where witches and sorceresses danced around a blazing bonfire singing ancient Celtic hymns.

# *"Will You Haunt Me?"*

A few weeks before my mother's death, I was with her constantly, holding her hand and talking as she listened. As the daylight faded outside the windows, I summoned up enough courage to ask her a question that was burning inside me. "Mom?" I asked.

"Yes?" she replied in a slurred voice.

"Will you haunt me?"

She lay there looking at me, the pupils of her glassy eyes reflecting my face. Thinking to myself what an idiotic question this must have seemed, I suddenly saw myself morphing into myself as a small boy, then a troubled teen, and then back to the young man I actually was. "Yes." The answer both relieved and stunned me. I felt relieved that she answered me. I felt shocked because she said "Yes" and didn't seem to be joking.

In a sense, I guess I'm still "haunted" by her. I'm haunted by memories of my mother writing about me in the local paper, exposing my most embarrassing moments.

The night before we sold the house, I slept in the living room where she died, hoping her spirit would visit me. I rolled out a sleeping bag on the exact spot where she closed her eyes for the final time in our world. I lay patiently waiting for something, a sound, a bump, whatever. I closed my eyes and thought about her, envisioning her riding her three-wheeled bicycle through the air, all over the house, through every room. A rainstorm had come in from the ocean. Lightning cracked outside. Thunder interrupted the sounds of rain hitting the porch roof and waves breaking on the shore. This has to be the night, I thought. How perfect, my last night in the house and we have thunder, lightning, and rain. In my mind, I was ready for her to come and hover over me. She'd impart to me the wisdom of the ages. She'd be my Obi-Wan Kenobi, telling me that when I face a major challenge, "Use the force, Craigie."

I was prepared to hear anything she had to say, like "You were my favorite" or "I forgive you for hurling your jacket on top of the school's roof." I was ready for anything she was willing to share with me. Maybe she'd tell me I was going to be rich, famous, or that I'd live forever.

Nope, nothing like that happened. Matter of fact, she never appeared. I didn't even channel her through my dreams that night. I don't even think I dreamed anything. At least, when I woke up, I couldn't remember anything, except that she didn't come to visit me.

How could nothing have happened? I thought she told me she'd haunt me. Maybe she couldn't find me. It *is* a big universe, and there are a lot of people on our planet alone. Maybe she was just taking her time, or busy someplace else. I know she always wanted to go to Venice. Maybe she was in a gondola, writing heavenly poetry and drinking Italian red wine. It'll happen. She'll haunt me. I just know it. She told me so. But hey, let's be reasonable: if I was about to die and my son asked me, "Dad, will you haunt me?" I'd say, "Hell, yeah."

The kitchen was barren. All the plates, cups, and appliances were either sold, given away, or thrown out. Tara and I kept a couple of bowls for cereal in the morning. I walked into the kitchen after my uneventful night. Tara was pouring milk into her bowl of cereal.

"It didn't happen," I said.

"Huh? What didn't happen?" she asked.

"Mom didn't haunt me," I confided.

"Maybe she's waiting," she mused.

"Waiting…waiting…waiting for what?" I asked, puzzled.

"For the right time," she supposed.

"What's the right time?" I asked.

"You were waiting for her last night, right?" she asked. "Yeah," I said.

"Well, maybe she knew that, and she thought it wasn't the right time. Just because you thought it was the right time, that doesn't mean she thought it was the right time," she explained.

"You have a point there, I guess," I admitted.

"You were so sure that she was going to visit you last night. Maybe she wasn't prepared to visit you. Maybe you're not ready for her yet?" Tara said.

"I'm ready," I declared firmly.

"Oh, yeah, what makes you think so?" she questioned. "Libby was a smart lady and she knows when you're ready, so instead of waiting for it to happen, maybe just let it," she said. Tara's words sounded just like my mother's. Maybe, at that moment, my mother's spirit was talking through Tara and telling me to settle down.

# The New Owner

We sold the house to a guy who peddled Hawaiian shirts out of Philadelphia. He had made a lot of money. He was looking to settle down on the Jersey shore. He told me the house was "perfect." When Tara and I came back a year after my mom died for the summer, occasionally, I'd ride my bike down Jefferson Street and pass by the house. He and his wife sat outside the newly painted porch drinking wine and eating crackers. I'd try to ride by inconspicuously, but they'd always see me and ask me to come up for a drink. I'd politely make some excuse. I just couldn't go into that house and see a different carpet in the living room, an uncluttered attic without dust, a dining room with a dining table and chairs instead of hospital gear—reality in place of memories.

# Riding on Handlebars

Before leaving Cape May that summer, we had an early dinner with a friend who had a place on Jefferson Street. We ate salad in her small hot kitchen, talked about Cape May, and departed early enough to watch the sunset. Tara sat on the handlebars of my bike. We rode down the street. We passed by our old house. They'd painted the porch pink and I couldn't keep my eyes off of it. I hit a pothole in the street and Tara fell off the handlebars. She sat up on her butt and snorted, "You idiot, why did you do that?"

"I'm sorry. God, I'm sorry. I was looking at the house."

"Pay attention," she demanded.

"Are you ok?" I asked.

"No…yes, that just hurt," she exclaimed.

"I'm sorry."

"Just watch where you're going," she yelled. She brushed off her hands and knees.

The Hawaiian shirt guy came running out and said, "Tara, Craig, is that you guys? We saw you crash out front. Are you okay?"

Tara looked up and said disgustedly, "Maybe if Craig would watch where he was going, this wouldn't happen."

"Why don't you come into the house and get washed up?" he offered.

"No, that's ok," I said curtly.

"He's not talking to you, you knucklehead. I'm the one who fell, not you," she said. "Sure I'll go in and get washed up."

"I'll just wait here," I muttered.

"Come on in, we'll have a glass of wine," he offered.

"No thanks, we really have to get going. I'll just wait outside here. You go Tara."

I waited outside, staring down the driveway toward the garage. I wheeled my bike near the garage, stepped up on the seat, and peered into the window. The garage was clean—no clutter, no piled-up bikes, no old surfboards. It contained lawn furniture and other stuff suburbanites keep in garages.

Tara was in there for over fifteen minutes. I began to wonder what she was doing. I began to daydream. Maybe they kidnapped her. Maybe she's a hostage. Maybe I should break into the house and put that little guy with the Hawaiian shirt in a bear hug and demand to know her whereabouts. "Where is she?" I'd demand.

"I don't know what you're talking about," he'd say.

"Come on, I know you bought the house just to kidnap her. If you don't tell me where she is, I'll squeeze you until your head pops off."

And he'd say, "Let me go, you putz. She's cleaning her cuts because you were daydreaming about your long lost home. Well, it's gone buddy. I've got it now and there's nothing you can do about it."

Suddenly, reality intruded: "Craig, Craig, Craig...Craig. Come in here. I want to show you something."

It was Tara's voice. Up the brick steps I went, walking slowly from Craig's dream world to the real one. "What do you want me to see?" I asked in an out-of-it tone.

"George has something to tell you," she said excitedly.

"What do you want to tell me?" I asked, annoyed that I was being coerced into the house.

"There is something going on in this house and I need to know a couple of things," said George.

A precooked answer popped into my mind: "Listen man, this is an old house and we told you that when you bought it. Whatever is going on with it is what you get. We're not going to give you back your money or anything." Instead, I said something innocuous that I can't remember.

Then he said, "No, you don't understand. We love the house. It's just what we wanted. But something strange is going on here."

"Strange? What do you mean strange?" I asked.

"I think it's electrical," he said.

"Yeah, I know," I shrugged.

"What?" he asked.

"The Ayatollah wired it backwards, after we first moved in, so there's always shorts and stuff," I tried to explain.

George looked puzzled and asked, "Who the hell is the Ayatollah?"

"That's my father."

"Anyway, that's not it. It's something else."

He asked me to accompany him to the second floor. I did. Some of the stairs still creaked the way they did when I was a little boy trying to sneak out of the house and play Jailbreak. Tara, George, and I walked to the top of the steps and turned into the room that had been my mom's old home office. George flipped the light switch on and off.

"Lights turn 'on' and 'off' throughout the night," he said. "Sometimes, I know I turned them 'off' but they are 'on'. It can't be a short circuit because it's not just the bulb going 'on' and 'off' by itself. When I look, the switch is up when I know it was down, and other times the switch is down when I know it was up."

"That is strange," I said.

"And there's more," he continued. "Doors close and open every once in a while, while nobody is near them. I'm curious, did you ever experience anything like this?"

"I'm not sure," I said. "We always kidded that at Christmas time a ghost named Fred came to visit. My mom told my brother and me Fred came because there was so much joy in the air at that time. But I don't recall Fred turning the lights off and on, or opening and closing doors."

We had never told him that my mother died in this house. It's not something real estate agents encourage, our realtor told us.

"Are you scared?" I asked.

"No, I'm not, just curious," said George.

"Maybe whatever is in here with us is just being playful."

Undoubtedly, I thought.

We descended the stairs, walked out the front door, and waved. "So long. See you next summer."

Tara refused to get back onto the handlebars of my bike. We walked toward the beach, having missed the sunset. What we hadn't missed was something brighter.

> "I've written a kind of humor column for umpteen or so years. People think I manage to laugh at the darndest things. Sometimes, many times, most times, those things are just a hair away from tears.
>
> Even the saddest moments can be a little funny and the funny moments, alas, can be a little sad. Who knows where the difference really lies?"
> —"Joyride" II, January 7 1981

# Epilogue

In preparation for writing this book, I read hundreds of my mother's personal memoirs, columns, and poems, along with notes she made to herself. Often, as she sat down to write her weekly column, my mom didn't know what she was going to write about. But as she began to bang away on her typewriter, she usually didn't have much trouble coming up with a town-related story involving her family and herself.

My relationship with my mother has come full circle. The journey I've taken is not something I wanted, nor something I expected. It was, however, for me, a valuable learning experience. By experiencing some of what she experienced, I have developed a deeper appreciation of my mother and her philosophy. I've learned the importance of living life to the fullest. I've learned to roll with the punches. One of my mother's favorite sayings was the title of a book by Erma Bombeck, a fellow newspaper columnist. It was *When Life Hands You A Lemon, Make Lemonade.* Now I understand why.

I've learned that "the little things" actually are the most important things. I've come to acknowledge the sacrifice and kindness of most caregivers, and the insensitivity and carelessness of a few. I've to come recognize the splendor of the world around us, and that suffering does not have to be meaningless. I've come to perceive that my mother's spirit continues to offer me guidance and, on occasion, protection. Though no longer here physically, in a very real sense, she continues to be present for me and, I suppose, for others. Her love remains. My love for her also remains. Such love never dies.

978-0-595-33816-0
0-595-33816-X

Printed in the United States
28676LVS00001B/7